The High Society

Drugs and the Irish Middle Class

The High Society

Drugs and the Irish Middle Class

Justine Delaney Wilson

Gill & Macmillan

Gill & Macmillan Ltd
Hume Avenue, Park West, Dublin 12
with associated companies throughout the world
www.gillmacmillan.ie

© Justine Delaney Wilson 2007
978 07171 4178 4

Typography design by Make Communication
Print origination by Carole Lynch
Printed by ColourBooks Ltd, Dublin

This book is typeset in Linotype Minion and Neue Helvetica.

The paper used in this book comes from the wood pulp of
managed forests. For every tree felled, at least one tree is
planted, thereby renewing natural resources.

A CIP catalogue record for this book is available
from the British Library.

5 4 3 2 1

For my boys
Matthew, Morgan and Reuben

Contents

Preface

> 'Nothing is illegal when 100 businessmen decide
> to do it.'
>
> FRANK, DRUG DEALER TO DUBLIN LAW FIRM

In May 2003, I was part of a production team that worked on a documentary for Irish television purporting to show the reality of drug abuse in this country.

As part of my research for the programme I spent three days in two locations considered to be havens of the illicit-drug trade in Dublin. Both were flat complexes; one in Ballymun, the other on Sheriff Street in the north inner city. Every hour of each day and night, I witnessed a constant stream of young people in and out of filthy stairwells and grotty rooms, buying their gear. The same hooded faces appeared again and again in every single twelve-hour period.

In the meantime they would have gone 'on the rob' before appearing back for another fix of coke or heroin. Small-time dealers would buy bigger amounts to sell on. Over the six days the steady trade in drugs in both locations was astonishing. A lot of money was being made.

On a sunny Tuesday morning in July 2006, I accompanied a very handsome and well-dressed forty-one-year-old man into the offices of one of our most highly respected and long-established city centre law firms. It was my first time through the big glass doors, which he has been walking through twice weekly for the last nine years.

Carrying an expensive leather bag, he greeted the receptionist and they exchanged familiar pleasantries. He knew his way around and went straight to the lift. She didn't ask him who he was there to see. Perhaps she knew, or knew not to ask. The summer sun streamed into the lobby where I waited in one of those leather couches that looked inviting but was next to impossible to get out of. That I was waiting for a dealer wasn't really that shocking. That I was waiting in the lobby of one of the capital's top law firms was.

Within twenty minutes my companion reappeared from the lift and we left the building. On the way in, his bag had contained heroin, cocaine, hash and ecstasy (MDMA) divided into small packages with codes on them. On the way out, it contained €17,600.00 in cash.

More money changed hands in those twenty minutes in that beautiful glass building than around the clock in three days in a flat complex in Ballymun and three days on Sheriff Street.

Acknowledgments

I am very grateful to the many men and women who spoke to me over the last year for this work; in particular, to the drug users and recovering addicts who shared their personal experiences with me for inclusion in this book. They did so voluntarily and with the understanding that their accounts might be of interest to others in a similar situation and might help shake the rest of us out of our collective denial.

Thanks also to the following who gave of their time and expertise:

Dr John O'Connor, Clinical Director of the Drug Treatment Centre Board and Medical Director of the Rutland Centre

John Lonergan, Governor of Mountjoy Prison

Stephen Rowen, Clinical Director of the Rutland Centre

Rolande Anderson, Addiction Counsellor

Gerry Hickey, Psychotherapist and Counsellor

Dr Tom Lacey, GP and Addiction Counsellor

Dr Andree Rochfort, Director of the Irish College of General Practitioners (ICGP) Health in Practice Programme and ICGP Representative of the National Committee of the Sick Doctors Scheme

Colin O'Driscoll, Senior Psychotherapist at Forest Treatment Centre

Detective Superintendent Barry O'Brien, Garda National Drugs Unit

Dr Aiden Meade, Chairman of the Sick Doctors Scheme

Johnny Connolly, Drug Misuse Research Division of the Health Research Board, author of 'Drugs and Crime in Ireland. Overview 3' (Health Research Board 2006)

The many Narcotics Anonymous members around the country.

Author's Note

A stereotype exists of the typical drug user: badly motivated, weak-willed individuals with poor academic records, irresponsible young people from underprivileged backgrounds, with little by way of religious conviction or self-esteem—the 'wrong sort'.

Of course, we accept that there are also 'recreational' users who are perhaps the 'right sort'. The social glitterati, the rock stars, the models and the fashionistas: all in possession of time, money and a penchant for coke on a Saturday night. We believe that beyond the back pages of the Sunday papers, such people have little bearing on our lives.

This book is an effort to confront these usual images and stereotypes by presenting the stories of a wide and varied group of professional people who are drug abusers and recovering addicts. Their stories challenge any glib and mistaken assumptions. Some may anger and horrify you. These are people from all sections of what is seen as respectable society—people with whom we all come into contact. Among them are law makers and law enforcers, politicians and accountants, doctors and surgeons, priests and nuns. They are individuals whom we hold up as being reliable, accountable and worthy of our trust. Shouldn't they—with their education and their advantageous position in our society—know better than to let us down in this way? The 'professional' drug abuser—of whom there are many—forces us to re-examine our attitudes towards, and our awareness of, both the drugs and the addicted around us.

Over the course of my research I interviewed fifty-two individuals who are drug users, dealers or recovering addicts. Of these, thirty-seven wished to have their stories included in the collection.

The majority of our meetings were recorded digitally—with the consent of the respective interviewees. A number of contributors preferred not to be taped. In these instances, I recorded the details of their stories on paper—with their consent.

In view of the sensitive and controversial nature of their stories, and the potentially career-damaging effects of telling them, I have protected the identity of those who spoke to me and that of their homes and places of work—hospitals, offices, court houses, schools, etc. However, the truth of their experiences and the integrity of their voices remain intact. One belief they all share is that drug use is not class specific.

One contributor told me that I'm like a priest writing about sex; drug abuse is something I haven't experienced firsthand. I hope this means that I have succeeded in presenting these stories without judgment and with some detachment.

JUSTINE DELANEY WILSON

JULY 2007

A Guide to the Gear

Nitrous oxide *laughing gas*
Nitrous oxide is a colourless, sweet-smelling gas that has a variety of uses. In the medical profession, nitrous oxide is most commonly used for minor oral surgery and dental work. It is also sold in supermarkets in small canisters, used to whip cream. Users inhale it through the mouth or suck it from a canister or a larger cylinder. Recreational abuse of this gas is on the rise in Ireland.

Persons experiencing a nitrous oxide high may have slurred speech and difficulty maintaining their balance. They would also usually be slow to respond to questions and immune to stimuli such as pain or loud noises.

Codeine
Codeine is derived from opium or morphine. A pain reliever and cough suppressant, it is widely available over-the-counter in chemists and usually taken orally in pill form, dissolved in water, or as a cough syrup. Codeine is one-fifth the strength of morphine and, as tolerance to it develops quickly, more is needed to achieve an effect.

When taken in high doses, codeine gives rise to a sense of euphoria and restlessness. The effects are felt within twenty minutes and last for one or two hours. Withdrawal includes flu-like symptoms such as aching muscles, hot flushes, anxiety, sleep disruption and loss of appetite.

Tranquillisers *downers, bennys*
There are thousands of prescription tranquillisers on the market and most often they come in tablet or capsule form. Many are ben-

zodiazepines, the most common of which are Flunitrazepam, Diazepam, Lorazepam and Temazepam. Xanax and Valium have long been popular choices among females. They are often circulated on the black market among addicts.

Tranquillisers reduce stress and anxiety and induce sleep. They can be addictive, and overdosing can be very dangerous.

LSD *acid*

LSD is a hallucinogenic drug and usually takes the form of little tablets known as *dots* or *tabs* in or on small squares of cardboard. These tabs may have logos or pictures on them. They are taken orally and, about an hour later, they result in a *trip*. The user's environment will appear to be different, with colours, sounds and objects seeming to be abnormal. The person may hear voices and see visions. The effects can last for several hours. If people have a 'bad trip', they may feel frightened, like they are losing control or going mad.

Magic mushrooms

Magic mushrooms are hallucinogenic mushrooms that grow in the wild. They can be eaten raw or cooked or made into a tea. The effects are similar to a mild, shorter LSD trip.

Poppers

Poppers are chemicals that come in liquid form, usually in small bottles. The vapour is inhaled and causes a rush which lasts for about five minutes. The blood pressure falls and the heart pumps faster. They can give rise to an increase in sexual arousal and a greater enjoyment of music and dancing.

Solvents

Solvent abuse is most often seen among teenagers. Commonly abused solvents include glue, paint thinner, nail polish remover, lighter fuels and deodorants. They are usually inhaled from a soaked cloth, a jumper sleeve, a bag or a bottle. Aerosols might also be sprayed directly into the mouth. Inhaling solvents gives a high which is similar to feeling drunk, dizzy and drowsy. The effects usually wear off within half an hour.

There is usually a hangover afterwards. The user may have a headache, may vomit or suffer a blackout. In extreme and rare cases, solvent inhalation can be fatal.

Amphetamines *speed, uppers*

Amphetamines are a group of stimulant drugs that usually come as a white-grey powder sold in folded paper packets—*wraps*. They are often referred to as the poor man's cocaine. Usually taken orally or snorted, they might sometimes also be injected. Another form, known as *ice* or *crystal*, can be smoked. They can make the user feel alert, talkative and overactive and may give a pleasure rush.

Most users feel a crash after the high. High doses can cause panic, paranoia and hallucinations. Amphetamines are psychologically addictive.

MDMA (methylenedioxy-N-methylamphetamine) *ecstasy, E, X, XTC, yokes, shamrocks, doves, Mitsubishis*

MDMA (most commonly known by its street name ecstasy) stimulates the secretion of large amounts of serotonin, dopamine and noradrenaline in the brain. This causes a general sense of openness, energy and euphoria. Users feel more alert, energetic, happy and have good feelings toward other people. Sounds, emotions and colours are more intense. It is used in some countries to treat post-traumatic stress disorder.

Ecstasy is commonly produced in back-street laboratories in a number of European countries. It is sold mainly as tablets with different designs and logos on them. Ecstasy tablets often contain other drugs and substances. Ecstasy may also occur in crystal form.

It can cause a rise in body temperature, blood pressure and heart-rate. Some people experience severe sweating, tremors and palpitations because of the increased cardiac load experienced. They may feel confused and dehydrated. Regular weekend users can experience a midweek crash that leaves them feeling depressed for days.

Ketamine *Special K, Kit-Kat, vitamin K, cat Valium*
Ketamine is a powerful, legal tranquilliser and anaesthetic used commonly by vets. Normally found in injectable form, it is converted into a powder or into tablets for human consumption. It is then usually taken orally or snorted.

A large dose will often cause hallucinations and blackouts.

Cannabis *hash, dope, grass, weed, blow*
Cannabis is a natural plant and is used in two main forms. The most common type is called resin, which appears as dark lumps or blocks. Not as common are the leaves and stalks of the plant, usually called *grass* or *weed*. Cannabis is generally rolled with tobacco into a *joint* or *spliff* and smoked, but it may also be cooked and then eaten. Getting stoned makes users feel relaxed and happy. Time seems to slow down and sounds, colours and tastes may be appreciated more.

Cannabis can affect memory and concentration. It is largely considered to be a safe drug but research shows it to be addictive. It increases the risk of heart disease and some cancers and may affect fertility. In Ireland it is the most common drug found in the systems of 'drunk' drivers, after alcohol.

Cocaine *coke, Charlie, snow*
Cocaine is a white powder made from the leaves of the coca plant, which grows mainly in South America. It is usually snorted up the nose, but can also be injected. It is a powerful stimulant and the effects last for up to twenty minutes after each use.

The depression that follows a high can be severe. With long-term or binge use, the effect of excitement can turn to restlessness, sleep loss, weight loss and paranoia. High doses have been known to result in heart attacks and blood clots.

Crack cocaine *rock, stone, free-base*
A more addictive form of cocaine, it is usually smoked. Smoking crack gives a shorter but more intense high than cocaine.

Heroin *H, gear, smack, junk*
Heroin is made from morphine, one of the opiate drugs that derive from the opium poppy. It is used by injecting or by smoking—known as *chasing the dragon*. Injecting heroin gives an immediate rush of excitement followed by a dreamlike feeling. The user feels relaxed, warm and drowsy. Pain, aggression, stress and sexual drive are all much reduced.

Heroin causes weak breathing and constipation. The real dangers, however, come from overdose and the risks associated with injecting. Physical and psychological addiction to heroin is the most common result of regular use.

Formerly the drug of choice of the working classes only, recent signs suggest that heroin is managing to make inroads into the lucrative middle-class market in Ireland.

Methadone
Methadone can be used as a heroin replacement drug to treat heroin addiction. It comes in the form of a green liquid, which people drink once a day to curb the cravings for heroin. The most serious risk from methadone is death by overdose.

A List of the Help

The Rutland Centre
Knocklyon Road, Templeogue, Dublin 16
www.rutlandcentre.ie
tel: 01 494 6358
Since it was founded in 1978, Rutland has grown into the largest private alcohol and drug rehabilitation centre in Ireland. It runs a drug-free programme, and no mood-altering medication is used. The centre provides a six-week residential treatment programme and continuing aftercare.

The Drug Treatment Centre Board (DTCB)
Trinity Court, 30–31 Pearse Street, Dublin 2
www.addictionireland.ie
tel: 01 648 8600
The DTCB is the longest established treatment service in Ireland. Originally located in Dublin's Jervis Street Hospital, it is now based at Trinity Court. It receives its funds through the Eastern Regional Health Authority. All out-patient facilities are provided on site. In-patient detoxification facilities are located at Beaumont and Cherry Orchard Hospitals.

The DTCB provides prevention, treatment, rehabilitation and aftercare programmes and also houses the National Drug Analysis Laboratory.

Narcotics Anonymous (NA)
www.na.ireland.org
tel: 01 672 8000
NA has only one mission: to provide an environment in which addicts can help one another to stop using drugs and find a new

way to live. Principles incorporated within the Twelve Steps of NA include:

- Admitting there is a problem
- Seeking help
- Engaging in a thorough self-examination
- Making amends for harm done
- Helping other drug addicts who want to recover

Forest
Co. Wicklow
www.forest.ie
tel: 01 201 5863
Forest is a new, private, therapeutic centre which offers a confidential service for people with alcohol or chemical dependencies. It offers a number of different services:

- The Change Programme—a three-week residential stay
- The Executive Addiction Treatment Programme
- The Highly Private Option
- The Corporate Retainer

St John of God Hospital, Stillorgan, Co. Dublin
tel: 01 288 1781
The mission of St John of God Hospital is to provide people who have mental health difficulties with an environment conducive to their healing, along with programmes of rehabilitation, care and treatment which facilitate their recovery. A modern 210-bed general psychiatric hospital, it has specialist units for substance abusers.

The Sick Doctors Scheme
The Sick Doctors Scheme was founded in 1985 to meet the needs of doctors in practice who are victims of substance abuse. It was formed by representatives of the Irish Medical Organisation, the

Irish College of General Practitioners, the Irish College of Psychiatrists, and the GP Wives Association.

The Scheme offers financial and practical help to enable doctors actively in practice to get treatment in approved units by specialists in the field. Anonymity and absolute confidentiality are vital; hence the only information on the committee's activities is provided through its annual report.

Foundation funding was through the parent bodies, and current funding is from donations and interest on fund investment. The fund is a registered charity.

The Spiritual Care Centre Dzogchen Beara

Garranes, Allihies, West Cork
www.dzogchenbeara.org
tel: 027 73032

Dzogchen Beara is a Tibetan Buddhist Retreat Centre under the spiritual direction of Sogyal Rinpoche, author of *The Tibetan Book of Living and Dying*. The centre offers retreats, meditation classes, rest and renewal breaks and care retreats. Accommodation is provided in the farmhouse hotel or in self-catering cottages.

Cottonwood de Tucson

Arizona, USA
www.cottonwooddetucson.com
tel: 1800 877 4520
tel: 0044 207 486 6222 (London office)

The Cottonwood de Tucson treatment centre is located just outside the city limits of Tucson on a thirty-five-acre site in the foothills of the Sonoran Desert in Arizona. Treatment is holistic, catering for the body, mind and spirit. The facility has a swimming pool, basketball and volleyball courts and nature trails. The programme length of stay varies between four and six weeks. Adult programmes available include:

- Chemical Dependency (including Prescription Drugs)
- Medical Detoxification and Acupuncture
- Detoxification
- Depression
- Anger and Rage

Cottonwood has a European office based in central London, which provides aftercare for former patients of the Arizona facility and also recovery support groups.

Chapter 1
The People and the Drugs

THE PEOPLE

'The community of Finglas in Dublin is in shock and is braced for an escalation of drugs-related violence following the shooting of two men.

'Martin 'Marlo' Hyland, suspected to have been one of the biggest drug dealers in Ireland, was shot dead yesterday morning. But what has utterly horrified people across the country was the brutal murder of twenty-year-old plumber's apprentice Anthony Campbell.

'Campbell was working at the house where Hyland was staying when the killers arrived. It is believed that they happened upon the young worker unexpectedly in the course of their attack on Hyland. Campbell's employer had left him alone working in a downstairs room in the house where Hyland lay upstairs in bed. When he returned after buying food and drinks at a local shop, he found the apprentice and Hyland both dead.

> *'Hyland had been warned by Gardaí that his life*
> *was in danger. It is believed that he was a major*
> *supplier of cannabis, cocaine and heroin to drug*
> *gangs across the country. An entirely innocent party,*
> *Campbell was shot in the head by a handgun with*
> *a silencer attached.'*

How many journalists reporting on the drug-fuelled murder of twenty-year-old bystander Anthony Campbell on 12 December 2006 smoked a few joints that evening? The following Sunday morning at brunch, how many middle-class professionals reading about the tragedy of the innocent twenty-year-old were themselves on a comedown from the previous night's coke? How many Gardaí working tirelessly to bust drug suppliers like Hyland help themselves to some of the heroin they seize in the process?

In Ireland, we haven't come to terms with the fact that drugs are everywhere, in all social strata. Contrary to the comfortable belief that drug abuse is limited to lower socio-economic groups in the inner cities, drug use—heroin, cocaine, amphetamines, ecstasy, LSD, ketamine, hash—among the middle classes is widespread, and growing.

The abuse of drugs amongst the professional and the materially privileged—doctors, lawyers, accountants, pilots, barristers, the clergy, and judges—is facilitated by societal attitudes. The financial resources to support a habit, the lack of supervision or account-ability in the workplace, and—with respect to doctors, nurses, and Gardaí among others—the ready availability of substances means that the middle classes are more likely to sustain their dependency without fear of detection or responsibility.

Substance abuse among those in the professions gives rise to concern and controversy. We don't want to consider that the sur-geon performing our father's heart by-pass, or the pilot flying our teenage children on their school ski trip, or the solicitor handling our divorce, or the accountant looking after our tax returns, or the middle-aged woman teaching our seven-year-old five days a week might be as high as a kite or strung out while doing so.

Of course there is a danger when we expect our public representatives, our professionals and our educators to occupy a higher moral ground and be more sensible than the rest of us. However, it is fair for us to assume that the people making policy for a whole country and the people performing surgery on our loved ones and the people flying us to the sunshine are in a position to fulfil their roles with a clear mind and in their full senses. When we confront the possibility that this isn't always the case, then the scaffolding of our society seems more than a little shaky.

However, facts and figures remain elusive. Unlike the stereotypical lower-class, unemployed and unemployable drug abuser that we're comfortable to imagine, saving face and protecting reputations are most important among the middle-class population. Responding truthfully to surveys or questionnaires about drug use and chemical dependency or registering themselves or a family member for treatment as a 'Substance Abuser', are not.

'Nobody will believe this book,' notes Dr John O'Connor, Clinical Director of the Drug Treatment Centre Board and the Medical Director of the Rutland Centre. 'If you write that you have spoken with a dealer who sells drugs to the employees of an impressive office block on the right side of the city centre, and has been doing so for the last nine years, people reading it will not believe you. Of course it goes on, but people don't want to believe it. They'll choose not to believe you.'

Dr O'Connor goes on: 'Addiction is not just about addiction to a drug, it's about addiction to a lifestyle; the ritual of using, the social element, the fast lifestyle. If you work hard, you also have to play hard. So you have to get going on your weekend immediately after you leave the office and you have to maintain this level of "fun" over a couple of days. Get the drink and the drugs into you as quickly as possible; that's the growing mentality. The stability of a life without drugs can be seen as a boring and flat alternative.

'One difference between middle-class users and those from disadvantaged areas is that the former will be selective about the drug they use and the effect that they're looking for—at least at the start. The lower-class user will take whatever he can afford or get his hands on.'

The disadvantaged are unfairly treated and blamed for the drug problem in this country. It is estimated that 96 per cent of the prisoners in Mountjoy are from the lowest socio-economic groups. The chance of spending time in the crumbling 157-year-old prison increases dramatically for those born on certain streets and in certain areas. None of the people in this book—despite the fact that some have had serious scrapes with the law and all have been in possession of large quantities of drugs—have any criminal convictions. Our attention is rarely turned toward people in the community with the real money to fuel a booming drug trade.

John Lonergan has been Governor of Mountjoy for twenty-three years. This isn't news to him: 'The most striking thing has always been that in the prison system in Ireland, it's poor people who fill the prisons. White-collar professionals are not represented in prison at all. In fact, not only are they not represented in prison, they're not even represented in the criminal system. They're not being convicted, and why not? A huge amount of skullduggery goes on in Ireland.

'Drugs are illegal for everybody unless they're prescribed by a doctor, for all social classes. But the reality is that the people we target most—indeed almost solely—when we talk about drug abuse, are those from disadvantaged areas. We see that the gangland areas are lower class areas, yes, but most of the money is being contributed by, and made in, middle class Ireland. And very many of the people buying and using the drugs are middle- and upper-class professionals.

'When people from areas that are regarded as deprived and disadvantaged leave Mountjoy, they are the focus—there's no question about it—of Garda surveillance a lot more than a person from a better area. The area you live in, the reputation you have, all that sort of stuff has a huge bearing on the amount of leverage you have, on what amount of flexibility is given to you, on what amount of attention you get relative to other people. Without a doubt, nothing like the same level of monitoring and policing goes on in middle- or upper-class areas as does in the poor areas. The middle classes are treated very differently.

'Take two young people, just for example. If a young lad, eighteen or nineteen years old, gets into difficulty and he comes from a very deprived background, almost the first consideration is a term in detention or something. It's almost as if the system is saying, "I'll do you a favour, I'll send you into prison or into detention and you'll be saved from this horrible existence that you have and the potential damage it might cause you, and we'll cure you by sending you to St Pat's," never thinking that a criminal conviction is going to be a huge disadvantage. The opposite psychology automatically kicks in when it's a young lad from a privileged background. Every effort is made to stop him getting a conviction; the last thing we want to do is to give him a criminal conviction because look at the con-sequences for him: He can't go to America, he won't be able to do this and that. It'll follow him around forever.

'For the very rare middle-class person who comes through these doors, a sentence is a real penalty, socially, culturally, in terms of career and reputation, and also the sheer physical reality of it—like Johnny Cash singing about San Quentin—they're hating every single minute of it. And the consequences when they leave—the chat among the neighbours, in the office, at the golf club—are too much to contemplate.

'It's hard to know just how prevalent drug use is among the middle class. This group's denial plays a huge part in preventing the painting of an accurate picture. Admitting my actions, openly accepting that I have an addiction problem, I'm involved in corruption, in some small way I've contributed to the shooting of someone like Anthony Campbell—nobody's going to want to admit that. So instead, denial. Denial that I'm involved, denial that I'm addicted, denial that I'm impaired doing my job, denial that I'm being a bad parent, denial, denial, denial.

'Every time a person buys any illicit drugs they're contributing to a greater industry. We don't connect middle- and upper-class Ireland and their yuppie drug use with the very serious gangland, criminal element. But it is these educated people and their money that provides the oxygen for gun and gangland warfare. Major shipments of cannabis or cocaine in this country are more often than not accompanied by guns. There is a huge black market in Europe for guns.

'In America years ago, you would hear that the affluent used to do drugs and deal cocaine as part of their lavish dinner party evenings. And now that's going on here. I know some very powerful people—public representatives—who are regular users. My belief, and it's based on reliable information, is that the same culture is here and it's growing, and growing rapidly.

'I know cocaine is associated to some degree with jobs that are stressful and financial and all that, jobs where you'd be anxious a lot and have a lot of pressure on you. Obviously the weekend is the time for relaxing and this helps you to relax and feel good and take a break from the whole thing. These users are very conscious that it is an illegal pastime and that it's an illicit trade because they don't do it openly. And yet they don't connect it to the drugs trade that they hear reported on the news. It's amazing. Such blinkered vision and denial.

'I was in Schull last night, out at the coast, and they tell me there's tonnes of drugs there. In Schull! They're coming in off the boats with them. I'm amazed. It's such an outlying and rural area. The whole thing is amazing. It's an amazing world out there in terms of all the drugs right across this island in all social classes. What's amazing is that in little villages where there's only 100 or 200 houses, people are saying, "This place is awash with drugs now." Isn't it amazing?'

Gráinne Kenny, Founder and President of Europe Against Drugs (EURAD), feels strongly about adults who try to defend their use of cocaine and other drugs by classing themselves as 'only recreational' users: 'I've no time for the growing band of educated, middle-class, middle-aged people who are using drugs. They are involved in a highly dangerous and illegal activity, and somewhere down the line is a woman living in abject poverty who is being stuffed full of drugs and put on a plane to smuggle coke for the likes of him and his mates. The glorious promise of a job in a lap-dancing club is what she has ahead of her.'

Detective Superintendent Barry O'Brien of the Garda National Drugs Unit agrees: 'For somebody to access illicit drugs, someone else has to delve into organised crime in order to source it. But "respectable users" won't dwell on that. They won't see that they're contributing to crime in any way. They know this guy might be a bit dodgy but that's his business. It's the human condition to erect walls for ourselves and ignore what's behind them.

'One example of hypocrisy, where illicit drugs and ethics are concerned, are the drug users who are environmentalists—they recycle, they are eco-friendly and they are members of Greenpeace, and yet they'll consume amphetamines and other stimulants, which are creating major environmental hazards in places like Holland and Belgium where all the chemical waste product generated from their manufacture is being dumped into the rivers or driven into the forest and set on fire.

'Sorting their cardboard into green bins once a week isn't going to make up for this. Or perhaps they have a social conscience and believe that the situation in Latin America is dreadful, or the war in Iraq is illegal and unfounded. But they don't dwell on the fact that their habit is perpetuating a very nasty state of affairs in these places.'

Dr Tom Lacey (not his real name), himself a Narcotics Anonymous member and a practising doctor with thirty years experience treating people with addiction problems, believes that a large number of people of means who abuse drugs do so to ease some kind of pain: 'There's a perception that the only people who know what it is to truly suffer and to opt out of their lives are the working classes. The great majority of people with drug problems who make the TV or any publication are scumbags, or are portrayed as such.

'Any suffering that goes on in the middle or upper classes is often dismissed, because these people have money. "What have they got to whinge about?" Now that's utter nonsense. People suffer. It could be argued that middle-class suffering is possibly worse because you know that money can't alleviate it. At least the working classes exist with this false impression of wealth, this idea that if they had money, things could be different; if they won the Lotto their problems would vanish, or whatever.

'One of my addicted patients is very high up in a government department and is from a wealthy family. Money is no object, but it's also not going to solve any of his problems. Initially, drugs were his way out of his day-to-day misery. Now those original problems have been dwarfed by his severe chemical dependency.

'Very often there is a certain sense of belonging, even in your darkest moments, when you are working class and you have a drug problem. Granted, it may be the camaraderie of the damned to a degree, but it's something the doctor or the lawyer is unlikely to have with his neighbours or workmates.'

THE DRUGS

> *'I find this idea of drug "pushing" laughable. Pushing? It's far from pushing that drug dealers have to get involved in. Once word spreads that an individual is dealing drugs, he will be absolutely plagued by users with plenty of money, to the point that he'll have to turn them down many times, and switch off his phone. The dealer would need an unending and unlimited supply of the damn things if he was to even think about getting into pushing. Nobody needs to push drugs. It's a pull. The drug trade is based on the economics of pulling, rather than of pushing. Who would be pushing something that there's never enough of?'*
> COUNCILLOR LUKE FLANAGAN

> *'Speedballs—my favourite—coke and heroin as a combination. One is a sedative and one is a stimulant, so they hit all your centres at the same time and it's utterly overwhelming.'*
> RORY, BUSINESSMAN

At dinner parties, middle-aged hosts offer around cocaine and ketamine on a board once reserved for cheeses. Where once there was cream in the silver cream dispenser, now the cream has been done away with in favour of the inhalation of the gas itself from the canister.

It is rare to come across a person whose drug use is confined to one drug. However, when looking at the types of drugs used by our affluent classes, cocaine always manages to assume prominence. Historically, cocaine has been associated with the glamorous, frequently used by those in the Arts. The glamour and association of its use with money and success means that contemporary use of it in this booming nation is quite staggering.

In the US, cocaine consumption is down and the market is not as strong as previously. However, the European market is the fastest growing in the world. This country is more affluent than we ever imagined a decade ago. Our unemployment rate is at its lowest ever, and our drug use at its highest ever. We are the top of all European surveys on happiness, on the best places to live, and on drug use. We are living decadent lives: spending money, eating out, drinking and taking drugs like never before. With no indication that this nation is set to return to a time when few people could afford a drug habit, this is likely to continue.

Anecdotal evidence, coupled with the sheer amount of heroin on the streets in 'nice' areas, would suggest that heroin is currently being remarketed as a high-quality drug, with dealers making efforts to reclaim the market taken by the growth of cocaine use. Heroin with purity levels of above 50 per cent appeared regularly on the better streets of Irish cities in 2006. Traditional deals have been between 20 and 40 per cent purity. The single largest heroin seizure—118 lbs—in the history of this State occurred last October. Accepting the internationally recognised estimate that drugs seized by the police amount to a mere 10 per cent of what is actually available supports the belief that there has recently been a huge and sudden increase in heroin use in this country.

MDMA (ecstasy) is also enjoying unprecedented popularity. It gets you back on your feet quickly after a dinner party around at the neighbour's or after a night showing clients a good time.

'If you were using MDMA for the night, you could drink ten pints and still walk. Whereas, just alcohol—

ten pints? That's going to be a killer. You could sit out that hangover for thirty-six hours and eventually feel better, or you could go back again and after a line of coke or a few more [MDMA] crystals, you'd feel better. You'd be at your desk, ready for work in the morning, no problem. It's not much of a choice to make.'
LIAM JONES, ACCOUNTANT

The number of people hooked on prescription drugs is also rising dramatically. This is the result of several things, including the accessibility of illegal opiates through the Internet, the greater emphasis on pain control by doctors and the increasing number of people prepared to forge their own prescriptions. In 2001, only sixteen incidents of forged prescriptions were reported by the Gardaí. In 2004, this number had risen to 157 such offences. A nationwide study of 2,000 drivers suspected of intoxicated driving carried out in 2000 and 2001 identified a pattern of middle-aged drivers under the influence of benzodiazepine—a legally prescribed drug which impairs driving.

The recent rise in the abuse of the legal drug codeine is staggering, according to Dr John O'Connor. 'Walk into any pharmacy today and you will see that the biggest display is of Solpadeine. The Solpadeine display is highlighted and eye-catching; boxes of twenty-four. Lots and lots of people start "small" in this way. And if you look to the drug company, this product is its biggest seller— the biggest profit maker. In my experience, codeine addiction is about equal in terms of men and women and is most commonly seen in the middle classes. I would very often have two or three people at a time detoxifying off codeine in beds in Beaumont. Also, in the Rutland Centre, the number of people being admitted with codeine addiction has risen just as much as those presenting for cocaine abuse has.'

Stephen Rowen is the Clinical Director of the Rutland Centre in Dublin: 'They used to say that alcoholism was caused by poverty in Ireland, by joblessness, the cold damp weather, the lack of hope, the fact that the people of Ireland felt emasculated and all of that. Now we blame growing drug use on our prosperity; people have lost their roots, we're not connected to the land, we've too much money in our pockets, kids have too much freedom.

'All I know is that drug abuse is an equal opportunities destroyer. It goes after all kinds of people in all kinds of settings and your personal circumstances are no guarantee that you will or won't make it through.

'Heroin addiction in Ireland is an interesting phenomenon because from the mid-1980s until just a few years ago it was very much the drug of choice for folks from the culture of poverty and addiction, the lower income groups, the north inner city in particular, the south inner city, north Clondalkin, Neilstown, Jobstown—very specific areas.

'Cannabis was considered a soft drug, and while there were some ugly, horrible deaths from people overheating and dying from contaminated ecstasy on the rave scene in the 1990s, for the most part the "drug problem" was actually a heroin problem, and it was a Dublin problem, and in turn, Dubliners looked at it as mostly an inner-city problem.

'What we're finding in the last couple of years is pockets of heroin users in provincial towns like Athlone, Carlow, Tullamore, Arklow and places like that. And the users aren't working class. Heroin's making a comeback. Even among the idle rich.

'Drugs are a funny thing. Different ones come in and go out of fashion; different places too. There's a treatment centre in Arizona called Cottonwood and they get referrals from the British Isles. The referrals are almost all heroin and are all from the aristocratic upper echelon of society on this side of the water. In this way, sometimes a treatment centre will capture a certain niche of people. According to the Medical Director of Cottonwood, heroin has recently taken a foothold among the aristocratic set.

'Heroin is much more physiologically addictive than cocaine. Heroin gets into every cell in the body, so when the cells of your body are deprived of it, you get sick. Coke doesn't have the physical addictive power—nicotine is far more addictive—but it's such a great rush that people become very, very hooked on it. When it first came out here about thirty years ago we were told it wasn't addictive, but that psychologically you can get highly dependent on it. It's just so destructive that you couldn't call it anything but addiction, in my view.

'Users get this rush with cocaine and then they stop using and they crash—the cocaine crash—and only cocaine will bring them back up again. People talk about cocaine like it's this awesome feeling of power and self-confidence, feeling good and feeling confident and feeling empowered, "I'm in charge"; it's a great feeling. Then they stop using it and crash into a black hole. The craving is not for a physical satiation of the cells of the body looking for relief. It's rather a need to get out of the dark and depressive pit and back to the confidence.

'It is seductive and it's powerful. People say it's the best craic they've ever had, the best sex they've ever had, the best time they ever had, the best fun, it's just great!

'When you use cocaine, you don't run out of steam; its an accelerant, it's a stimulant, it wakes you up, you have more energy. And you need less sleep, so then you can drink more. Of course, when you drink more, you are more disinhibited in terms of sexual adventures. Cocaine is huge in this country. In about three or four short years, cocaine took off in every corner of this country. It's available in small villages, small towns, big towns, the north-west of Ireland, the south-east of Ireland, everywhere. There are people in here with cocaine habits that cost them €800 a day.

'Of course, among all of the horror stories and hysteria, the important thing to remember is that most people using cocaine are not getting hooked. If you have a group of seven or eight people and they all party with cocaine every so often, probably one or two will get hooked. Six or seven won't. They've been using it for years and they get off on it on Saturday nights. That's it. Not everybody who uses cocaine is going to become addicted, anymore than everyone who drinks is going to become addicted to alcohol. But we don't have a way of taking a blood test, of looking at somebody's DNA code, and identifying which is the one who will.

'If everybody's life went totally belly-up overnight within minutes of using their first line of coke, then nobody would use it. The fact is that there are a lot of people who do get away with using it over long periods; there are others who appear to get away with it but eventually fall apart; and then there are those who seem to be in trouble from the first line.

'There are times when global politics affect illicit drug supplies around the world. For example, during the Afghan war when the American troops were invading, heroin supply was severely affected. A huge percentage of the world's poppy heroin supply ultimately comes from Afghanistan, so supply was restricted for a while and it drove up the price.

'We get a lot of people into Rutland who are using over-the-counter medication. Of all the products that you find in a chemist, the two most popular in terms of volume sales are Solpadeine and Nurofen Plus, both of which contain codeine. There's an awful lot of codeine abuse in people who are very middle class. It's a morphine. You get a real buzz from it, you get to float on a euphoric cloud, nothing bothers you, you just float. Let's face it; life is stressful, for everybody, you, me, everybody. You don't have to be stressed with codeine, you just float.

'Sometimes a codeine abuser will ring us: "I can't live this way and yet I can't get through a day or a half day without a couple of boxes of Nurofen Plus or Solpadeine." The cravings are so bad and they say they feel like a slave, they feel like they are in solitary confinement, they can't live until they get their hands on these tablets. Like Johnny Cash in the movie grabbing for the tablets. People feel trapped and they don't want to be trapped anymore. It's also not unusual for us to get a call from the partner or the parents of a person who is in trouble in this way.

'That said, I'm not sure that the majority of people who abuse over-the-counter pills ever hit a wall. They play this game for life. They adjust their budget—the way a lot of people spend a couple of thousand a year on tobacco and another couple of thousand a year on alcohol. They get used to spending their money on pain pills, just as most people who use coke every Saturday night account for it in their weekend budget.'

'In a room where people are using cocaine, the atmosphere crackles,' says Dr Tom Lacey. 'Some people find that uncomfortable while others find it exciting. Cocaine people come at you; they're snappy, snappy.

'For middle-aged people who have made money, those who are still on the treadmill, cocaine is initially a godsend because it enables them to spark like the younger people, which is something they feel they could not do naturally. I'm sick of listening to one person after another telling me they are only recreational users. Telling me they're handling it, they're just using at the weekend. I don't give them the tired old arguments about progression or wag the finger. I need to be there when they fall. I think ahead to eight months down the line, or so, when they invariably come back in complaining about money.

'Money is often the first problem with cocaine, not health. You can never have enough coke or enough money to pay for it. I watch patients of mine, prominent people with great incomes, running up massive debts. Paying for coke, buying the cars and the houses and glamorous trappings that go with that scene, then crashing the bloody cars . . .

'They say that cocaine is God's way of telling you that you've too much money, and I tend to believe that. It's also very bad value, any way you look at it; it's a bottomless pit and it makes hard bargains with you. There may be some people out there who really manage to remain occasional cocaine users, but in all my time I have never met any of them. And I'm thirty years sitting here listening to all sorts.

'Heroin has been déclassé since the early 1990s. It hasn't been cool, although I hear it's getting madeover and may be set to make a comeback. God help us if it does.'

Rolande Anderson is an addiction counsellor with vast experience. He is involved in training with the Irish College of General Practitioners and in private practice. Previously he worked for almost twenty years in St Patrick's Hospital in Dublin and he has also been Assistant Director in the Rutland Centre.

'From what I've seen, I would say that addiction to prescription drugs—Valium, Librium and Xanax—is among the most serious of all addictions. There is a huge black market for those drugs; lots of false prescriptions going around and it's really terribly serious. The over-the-counter stuff is very dangerous too: Solpadeine, Nurofen, all of those things. There are huge mark-ups for the people who sell them, but they're terribly dangerous and addictive because of the codeine.

'In every profession, there is an alcohol and drug problem. It's hidden, but it exists right across the board. A definite change lately is the increase in professional women presenting with drug-abuse difficulties. I see different addiction stories every day. There are common themes and threads, but all the stories and voices are different. And more and more, those voices are female.'

According to Rolande, testing for drugs in the workplace may not be the solution that many might think. 'The issue of agreeing to random sampling in your place of work is an interesting one.

My view on random testing is that it has to be right across the board. It has to be equally done and you have to be clear about what you are testing for, and what will be done about a positive result. It can be a nightmare to get an accurate result. What are the rules? If someone has taken a codeine tablet for a headache and turned up for work, what happens then? It is the most awful thing to have to do; humiliating for the person taking the test, mortifying for the person standing watching, forbidden from averting their eyes. There is no trust with this test; you have to get that out of the way from the start.

'Also, a lot of places won't have a chain of command that is safe enough for samples to be dealt with properly. A good example is pilots. Should pilots be sampled randomly for drugs? You're probably more at risk from the air hostess who doesn't close the door properly. And if you do get a positive result, what happens then? What are the policies for staff who have drugs in their system? Do you enroll them in, and support them through rehab? Are they fired on the spot? Rules can be very difficult; there are always exceptions and different cases.'

The use *per se* of drugs, excluding opium, is not a criminal offence in Ireland. The distinction between use and possession can lead to confusion in this area. Drug consumption or use refers to the mere *use* of illicit substances, and is separate from illicit acts such as possession, cultivation, transportation or supply. However, in practice, it is impossible to use a substance without first locating and possessing it, as the contributors to this book will now attest with their personal stories.

Chapter 2
Doctor and the Medics

'For a period of three years, the first thing I did when I got to work every day was use drugs. I would take fentanyl intravenously. It's a short-acting opiate—used widely for anaesthesia. I used it to get me through the day.

'I've been through treatment twice. The first time I relapsed after being clean for about four months. After that, I did worry that perhaps my position and place of work were inconsistent with recovery, but I was determined not to lose my career. Since coming out of treatment the second time, I haven't used at all. That was twenty months ago.'

MOLLY, FORTY-THREE, MEDICAL PRACTITIONER, WEST OF IRELAND

'We have had many doctors through the Rutland Centre for treatment. At any one time, we have twenty-four people in our six-week residential programme. One or two of these are often doctors—

GPs mainly. In the US it's accepted that, at the very
least, 10 per cent of doctors are substance abusers.
Is the figure the same in Ireland? I would expect so,
certainly. But they're not all going for treatment,
that's for sure.'
STEPHEN ROWEN, CLINICAL DIRECTOR OF THE
RUTLAND CENTRE

———

Talking about the widespread use of mood-altering drugs amongst
those in the professions will always cause concern and controversy,
and understandably this will be particularly heightened when the
profession we are referring to is the medical profession.

Michael is a consultant based at a North Dublin hospital. He
makes life-saving decisions every day of the week. None of his
patients knows that he is a daily drug user.

In addition to surgery and patient care, my responsibilities include
teaching and keeping up to date with current medical research,
among other things. I take methamphetamines to keep everything
under control; without my daily dose, I simply wouldn't get the job
done as efficiently.

I started about four years ago, taking just five milligrams, when
I had a particularly stressful or busy day. It has definitely made a
difference to my performance and the ease with which I get
through my workload. Now I take a fair bit more, maybe 30 milligrams a day. On the odd occasion, I've taken up to 50 milligrams
or so, but I find that it actually starts impairing my performance
then, and I worry about making potentially catastrophic mistakes.

I take tricyclic anti-depressants to combat the sleepiness and
lethargy that I feel on my rare days off. I have so little time for my

family that I need to be at my best when we all have free days to spend together.

——

According to Dr Andree Rochfort—Director of the Health in Practice Programme, a system of confidential health-care support for doctors with addiction problems—'doctors with drug-use difficulties are dealt with particularly harshly by society, and they get the worst time of all from their colleagues. It is just the worst profession in which to have a problem with drugs.

'We are part of the general population—us, the doctors. We are part of the mainstream, us middle classes. Of course we are as susceptible to angina, diabetes, depression and addiction as everyone else. Being trained in health-care does not mean we never get sick. Our medical knowledge does not confer immunity to stress or other problems.

'If you're a doctor and you're sick, your problem won't be resolved by going to a doctor like anyone else. Because you're a doctor, other medics don't ask the same questions; they take shortcuts in examinations; they might suggest the prescription you need but not write it. It would be expected that you write it. Your investigations or ultrasounds or whatever wouldn't be organised for you, there'd be little follow-up and you'd probably intercept any results yourself.

'It gets very difficult when we talk about mental health and addiction problems. One in six of the Irish population has a mental health problem, so we can expect that at least one in six doctors has a mental health difficulty. Many Irish doctors self-medicate for stress and depression and to help them to cope. What our particular job does to us in terms of workload, the expectations of patients and their loved ones, the expectations of the profession, peer pressure, illness all around us every day, the distress and the pain—it can all be an awful lot to bear. There is an emotional side to practising medicine, but this side is hidden. A doctor must not be seen to be upset. I'll hand you the box of Kleenex but I'll appear distant and solid. Over years, all of these issues can accumulate and take their toll.

'Prescription drugs are usually the chemical substance of choice with medics due to the obvious availability. They're freely got, compared to street drugs. It's very, very hard to get statistics of the instance of drug abuse among our profession in this country. It's a tightly closed area and not one that's likely to be talked about.

'It's not illegal to write a prescription for yourself. It's unethical and regarded as not best practice but it happens all the time. Doctors can also write prescriptions for someone else and take the medication themselves. Some pharmacists have cottoned on to various doctors' habits—perhaps if their prescriptions for certain preparations are very high. But for the most part a doctor won't be questioned.

'Problems of addiction can go on for seven to ten years before they're picked up. A pharmacist, a colleague in the practice, or a family member might eventually contact us to seek advice on what to do. That said, some families find it very difficult to admit to the addiction because their own status and standing in the community is involved. Oftentimes, it will turn out that patients suspected something. A doctor's work may have been affected, there may be all sorts of behavioural patterns, punctuality problems, there may be drowsiness or slurred speech or erratic behaviour or mistakes made, perhaps.

'From my experience, I know that a lot of doctors who've had problems with substance misuse feel they don't get much by way of compassion from their colleagues. Where their colleagues may well be compassionate towards their patients with problems like this, they feel that in some way they are regarded as having failed or as having let the profession down.

'Research shows that doctors who enter treatment programmes actually do better than the general population, partly as a result of the fact that they've put years into this career and because their own standing and that of their family largely depends on it. They are usually determined, intelligent individuals with the ability to rationalise this. They know there is a lot at stake if they don't succeed in treatment.'

———

'I remember the first day I found pages of old scripts in a drawer at home; he had been writing prescriptions for his elderly mother for pethidine and morphine and picking them up in various different chemists around. He was taking them intravenously and orally.'

Darcey Clarke is a medical consultant, as is her husband, Matt. He has been abusing drugs since medical school. Both Darcey and her husband are highly regarded in their respective professional fields. Despite his daily drug use, she has never reported him to the medical council or other regulatory body. She admits that the medical profession is possibly the most closed of all professions with regard to speaking up about addiction and taking action where doctors are known to be abusing substances. Silence and secrecy are the order of the day. 'I don't think those in power would thank you for bringing an impaired medic to their attention. They'd be forced to do something about him then,' she says.

Darcey and Matt are still married.

Matt managed to secure a consultant's post as a relatively young man; he has always performed well at work. The one thing he has always held onto is his ability to be controlled and clever at work despite any inward chaos.

I imagine his colleagues perceive him as being short-tempered and abrupt, but very good at what he does. These days, he's a creature of habit and routine. Over the years he started going in to work earlier and earlier, so now he gets to work before 7 a.m. and stays until just after lunch. More often than not, his afternoon comprises him injecting himself with drugs and going to bed for a couple of hours. Ordinarily I'm at work at this time, so he gets up later in the evening and, if the boys come around to visit, we all try to play not quite 'happy', but rather 'vaguely tolerant', families.

I go to bed at around 10 p.m. and he stays up and uses again. He might have a few drinks too. In the morning before he leaves for work, he uses drugs to get him going. I find needles around the house all of the time.

I think I became emotionally numb about everything except the children a long time ago. I have shut myself off from a lot of stuff. I've gone ahead with my career where I imagine I am considered tough and not very understanding. I think that's one of the problems that the medical profession suffers with; from the very beginning I think we have set ourselves slightly—for want of a better expression—on a pedestal, and everything in our training reinforces that. It's so competitive to get into medicine, and it's so competitive to stay in and stay on top of the job. It's competitive to get the training positions, it's competitive to get a consultant post and so on, so you're watching your back constantly not to make a wrong move. There is no way that you are going to be perceived as weak by looking for help, or in my case—particularly as a female consultant—admitting either that I had problems at home and was under stress, or that my husband was addicted to pethidine and various other substances.

There's no debriefing for doctors. If I've had a tough day where something horrible has happened or somebody young has died, there's no debriefing system for me anywhere along the line. So all the way along, doctors are carrying all of this. Always just coping and coping and coping, lurching from one bad day to another.

The Matt that I married was a very brilliant medical student. By the time of our wedding, he had just qualified. I didn't realise at that stage that he was helping himself to some of the medical supplies. I was young and innocent, and I suppose we tended to drink relatively heavily, as students do, and medical students possibly in particular. It wasn't really until a while after we got married that I realised that he would always have a drink or two before we went out. Again the penny didn't drop, in retrospect I don't know why— denial certainly forms a huge part of the spouse's take on things— but he became violent soon after our marriage.

The violence was intermittent at that time. The drinking continued and then the violence would be sparked off by the smallest thing. For example, I always kept my own name and his friends would tease him from time to time about how I wasn't conforming and did he not have any control over me?, … that wonderful 'rugby' attitude. He'd be livid with me when he got home.

And then we moved abroad for training and that's when he really started to deteriorate. There were needles all over the house and everything was denied and he was drinking more and more heavily. I knew the needles weren't work-related because we were both hospital-based and there was absolutely no need for such things at home. But of course one of the things about medicine is we obviously have access to drugs.

I remember being heavily pregnant at that stage and my brother-in-law coming to stay with us and Matt on the floor spaced out on whatever he'd taken. His brother and I had to drag him into a bed and all the while I was pleading and pleading with his brother not to tell anybody. So I was on the one hand denying it to myself, and on the other admitting it to myself but not wanting anybody else to know. I was keeping his secret.

I had always been very competent and the kind of person who got on with things. So I did everything that needed to be done. All he has ever had to do, basically, is survive his working day.

I didn't want to know the details of his substance abuse—absolutely not, no, no, no. And then when our first son was about eight months old, I have no idea what sparked it off, he became extremely violent. He had been taking drugs and he was out of it. He had some kind of a psychotic episode all geared at me and I fought for my life, literally. I still have bite marks on my arms. Eventually he passed out and I left with my baby son.

I drove like a lunatic to the airport and sat waiting for a flight to Dublin. I arrived into the parental home, babe in arms, early the next day. I sobbed on the plane, and I broke down completely when I arrived home and told my parents part of the story. I didn't mention the drugs—just the alcohol—and my father asked if he had been violent and I said: 'Yes, that's why I left.' At that stage, Matt had awoken from his stupor and was panicking looking for me. As far as I was concerned, that was it. It was over.

But my father, whom I loved and greatly respected, said he thought Matt deserved one more chance. So I went back. Defeated.

We were very isolated, I suppose, and medical hours were long. I'd be on call and I had a young child, so all of my time was pretty well taken up. I didn't have any time for confiding in friends. Most of my friends were doctors anyway, so I wouldn't have ever said a word. I'd have been making very serious allegations about another doctor, even though he was my husband. I also felt great shame among these friends—people I had graduated university with—shame in admitting that I had married a drug abuser.

I became pregnant again and over the years there were violent episodes. We were living in the States then. I gave up discussing anything about my marriage or my home life with my parents because I hadn't their support in the way that I would have wished. The support I needed that time I arrived into the house was 'Yes,

you're right. You're on to a non-winner here'. We both got consultant posts and there were dry periods from time to time, periods
where there seemed to be no drugs or alcohol. Those times were
okay.

I think he has only been publicly seen in a 'drunken' state—far
more likely to have been a drugged state—on two occasions ever.
All of his abuse is hidden and private. And I've helped in this. I've
always done all I can to keep it hidden. I didn't, and don't, confide
in anyone. I never dared to tell this story.

Professionally, there have never been any consequences of his
actions. I don't know, but over his career he must have misinterpreted
results or missed diagnoses, surely? Nothing's ever been traced
back to him though. I recall one afternoon, after we returned to
live and work in Dublin, he was in a really terrible state arriving
home from work. He passed out shortly after coming through the
door and I did feel duty-bound to phone the Medical Council, but
then the idea of the fallout from that for him and for me was too
much. I think the level of denial, secrecy and so on that you feel
when you're living with that level of addiction is very strong.

About eight years ago, I was under a lot of pressure at work
myself and I wanted him to move out. I couldn't stand it anymore.
His behaviour at home had become utterly unbearable and he was
very manipulative and very controlling. I had had enough of
walking on eggshells: 'I mustn't upset Matt, I mustn't disturb Matt.
I won't say anything inflammatory. I'll suppress what I really think
about such and such.' It was an emotional quagmire really, in that
everything was suppressed. The children were older and they knew
to walk on eggshells too. They'd been doing it all their lives.

There were never any moments of honesty between us. Never.
Addicted individuals will lie to you about anything and everything. There were periods when he'd promise me he'd never use
drugs again. I mean, we'd often have those kinds of conversations.
I believed it the first dozen times, but after that I didn't. Sometimes,

he'd be so convincing and make all kinds of declarations and I'd be quietly hopeful. But not anymore. He doesn't even bother making those false promises these days. We both know it's nonsense. But eight years ago—when I still had a little bit of fight left in me—and I'd come to the end of my tether, I wanted to get him out.

I still hadn't told anybody about it. We would have appeared to be the perfect family; two rather eminent doctors, teenage sons excelling in school. A beautiful house full of beautiful things, and yet at the heart of this life was absolute rot. Rot and distress and pain and fear. I think I was getting to the stage where I was probably clinically depressed. I'd gone to see one of my physician colleagues and said I was feeling rotten and my blood pressure was up. I said I'd been under a lot of stress. I didn't say why. The second time I went to see him, I just burst into tears and I told him I had problems at home. I was just pent up and tense and hyper and I'm sure if you looked into my face, it was distorted with sadness and rage. That day was the closest I've got in our married life to indicating that all was not rosy.

I wanted him to move out but he refused. He said he'd done nothing wrong and I couldn't take his sons: 'If you take my boys from me, I'll murder you.' I still have this letter where he actually wrote that down for me as some kind of warped promise and reminder. I fully believed him. I still do. I believe he is fully capable of doing that—coming after me and murdering me.

The boys were getting older. And I worried constantly about how they were being affected by the environment they were growing up in. The manipulation, the control, the tentacles tightening around everything, how he dominated our lives with his ominous, casually delivered threats. It's only now, looking back, that more and more I realise just how controlling he was and it's very difficult to describe.

Here I was in a senior position in a hospital, a very pressurised, very challenging and very rewarding job, trying to hold my family together and not talking to anybody. I hosted lots of family events and parties and all sorts of stuff. Everything appeared hunky dory, and if I socialised without Matt I'd make an excuse. My life was one big lie.

My eldest son came home one night about four years ago—at this stage he was in his twenties—and Matt was out of it downstairs. Rob challenged him and his father promised he'd never drink or use drugs again. Poor Rob believed him. He felt so betrayed when he found him using again two days later. Things have been pretty rocky for our entire marriage, but now I've cut myself off from him, emotionally. I live here and he lives here, and that's about all we have in common, our address. I don't feel any fear or anger, just immense disappointment at how my life has gone when I think about it. And huge sadness for my children, that they didn't have the stable and loving family upbringing that they deserved.

I became quite ill three years ago and I had pretty major surgery. It was very painful and very serious. I remember he came in to see me three days later. He was in bad form. I had just been helped into a special sitting-in bath, the ones you get showered in, and he said: 'Oh I don't feel well. I have a cold.' I remember thinking, 'You've got a *cold*?' I said: 'Why the fuck did you come and visit me? The only purpose of a visit is to make somebody feel better. I've had very serious surgery and I'm being washed by a woman half my age and you're complaining about your runny nose? Just go away.' This is the kind of complete disparity in perception that has always gone on. There has been no intimacy in our relationship over the last couple of years. The children have grown up and they've moved on.

A short time after my diagnosis late in 2003, he had a major breakdown and went into a treatment centre for six weeks. He came out of it full of hope and all full of evangelical drive for life. Everything was going to be wonderful and I was wonderful and he couldn't believe what he had put me through, blah, blah, blah.

I was very hopeful. I have a huge sense of family, even though that night when I took the flight with my baby I would have left him. But just then, after my surgery and his breakdown, I was willing to work with him, so we joined a two-year aftercare programme. At the first meeting, they said that people stop growing up at the time they start abusing substances. It turned out that Matt had started stealing alcohol from his parents' drinks cabinet when he was twelve. So I had married an adolescent. I was trying to keep it light, trying to maintain a sense of humour at the meeting, so I said I had married a twelve-year-old, was living with a fifteen-year-old and I was looking forward to him becoming nineteen or so. The others laughed but Matt was absolutely livid. I could see him clenching his jaw.

That was the end of that. He wouldn't go anymore. And he started drinking and using heavily again—if he had ever stopped . . . His evangelical glow burnt out that night.

One evening, a few weeks later, he was ready to strike out at me and I stood up as straight as I could and went towards him rather than away from him. I confronted him and said, 'You've no right to hit me or to push me around,' and he didn't. And he never did after that.

We had our one and only one marriage counselling session shortly after that episode, at my request, and it was completely obvious to everybody in the room, including myself, that we were going nowhere and that the relationship was dead. I detached myself fully from him then. For the first time, and for good.

I think in the early years, I was probably protecting myself as much as I was protecting him by not saying anything. You're so dependent—in the early years of medicine, you're so dependent—on your reference. It's very easy to stop somebody's career if there's any little black mark against them. This might include difficulties or distractions at home. It's not right, but that's the way it works. So you don't show any kind of weakness. I would have perceived it as a weakness that I had married an addict, and similarly I would have been displaying a weakness in looking for any help. I think that doctors, as a group, are particularly unwilling to go for help or to seek out help.

We have empathy with patients, we certainly do get affected by some of our patients, but I don't think we have emotional and feeling vocabulary. We've all the scientific evidence-based stuff and I think there is genuine empathy from most of us, but it's couched in terms like, 'We'll do the best we can for you and find out what's wrong'; that kind of stuff. The vocabulary to actually deal with feelings and real emotion is not there. I'm in an interesting position because I'm a doctor, I'm also a doctor's wife, an abused woman, the wife of an addict, and now I'm also a patient. I experience these things from every angle.

The road to get to consultant level or if you're in law, for example, barrister level or whatever, is such a rocky and aggressive road in many ways, that you just keep going and you don't have time for the feelings and emotions that maybe other people do. For female consultants in particular, it is important that you be perceived as tough. I think the professions are difficult places. Lots of jobs are tough for women. In professions that are traditionally dominated by men, by power and by money, the guys just don't want you having a slice of their cake. Even in this apparently enlightened era. A very eminent male doctor once told me that I was a power-monger because of the position I hold. He wouldn't have said that if I was a man.

Up until last year, Matt went through phases where he'd announce with a flourish that he was finished with all the drugs and the drink. But I didn't care anymore. I've little or no dealings with him and certainly no feelings. Anyway, I knew not to listen. At last. Because it's never been true.

He's an extremely intelligent and well-read man with a very powerful mind. I can only assume that's how he still gets through his working days. It's a miracle that he hasn't managed to seriously injure a patient in all the years he's practising. As far as I know, there has never been any sort of investigation into him or his behaviour. Of course, he is absolutely brilliant at lying and a master of denial so he'd be hard to pin down and very difficult to challenge. He'd put on his pin-stripe suit and stand upright.

To my knowledge there isn't a system within hospitals to report on a doctor you think is a 'sick' doctor. I think there may well be avenues through which you can express your concerns about other health-care professionals. For example, if you're worried about a nurse, you could go to the nursing director, but because we're individual practitioners and, rightly, I think, hang on to the independence of our individual decision making, then the buck stops with us. We don't have a regulatory body monitoring our behaviour.

In an impressive, detached house the walls are thicker and the neighbours further away. It is possible to keep a problem under wraps. I imagine that's more difficult if you live in a thin-walled flat. I think the higher up the social scale you are, the less likely you are to look for help and the more likely you are to hide.

I'd guess that I'm perceived as successful, domineering and overly assertive by my colleagues. They wouldn't have the slightest idea what goes on in my home and how little control I've had over my personal life. We coexist now, Matt and I, in and out. I mean, we eat our dinner in the same room on occasion. Both of my boys are adults now. I think if you spoke to them, you'd find they think their dad has contributed very little to our lives. Certainly very little that's positive.

———

'It's a very tough place to be, to be the spouse or partner of anyone with an addiction,' explains Rolande Anderson, addiction counsellor, 'because the focus is always on the problem itself and on the user. The spouse, who is suffering dreadfully too, perhaps also trying to protect children, gets a very bad deal.

'In particular, being the spouse of the GP in the community or the spouse of a consultant in the hospital—whom you know to be abusing drugs—is a very difficult space to be in. If you're married to a medic who is addicted, you experience a lot of fear. You're terrified that the secret will get out, they will lose their job, and the family its livelihood. Doctors do not admit their difficulties readily. There is a horror that the public will almost get pleasure in seeing the mighty fall. There is so much pressure on doctors and they are very much at risk for alcohol and drug problems for a variety of reasons, the availability of drugs being the key one and socialisation being another. Doctors tend to mix in their own groups, with other doctors and nurses, listening to difficult cases and medical problems all day. Also, the litigation threat for doctors is horrendous these days—they do something and they're in trouble; they do nothing and they're in trouble. There's definitely a fear of messing up; the stakes are so terribly high. In addition, there's a culture of heavy drinking in the training years, and this can become, for some, heavy drug use down the line. There is very little, if any, access to emotional support for doctors.

'Two issues arise when dealing with a doctor with a drug problem. Firstly, the patient's rights; the doctor is entitled to the same treatment and privacy as any other patient. However, doctors tend to get worse treatment because they "should know better". Secondly, there is an issue surrounding the closing of ranks within this profession. Would a doctor's colleagues, if and when they noticed the problem, say anything? There is a culture of secrecy, certainly.

'If you're the doctor with the problem, who are you going to go to? Traditionally, the last person would be another doctor because of a fear of being perceived as weak and unable to cope and being viewed and treated differently from then on.

'There are serious issues in terms of their own future, but also in terms of their patients' futures, i.e. the health of the general public who come to them for care. So when I meet a new client who is a medic, there are two strata: Yes, I want to help you and there is no reason why you cannot be working as you get better, but also you have to assure me that you are fit to do a job that carries such risk.'

———

Eve Muldoon is twenty-eight years old and works as a doctor in a hospital in the midlands. She is a recovering addict and has been clean for the last two years.

I started using cocaine when I was in my third year studying medicine at the College of Surgeons in Dublin. I was introduced to it socially and during that first year of use, I only indulged maybe nine or ten times, and in a very social context. In the following academic year, I started to use it at night too, to allow me to stay up and study. I noticed that I could get more done in less time with coke. It energised me. Now I was using it to get through my workload, to fit everything in, to maintain my social life. I was barely sleeping anymore. I had always felt under pressure at college, as though I was just scraping through exams, and I felt that at any time the whole thing would collapse because I wasn't as clever as the rest of them.

Now I was compulsive about studying and knowing as much as I could. I was depending on coke to give me an edge, and it did. For the first time, I was managing to keep up.

Soon after, I started my six-month post as a junior doctor in a hospital outside Dublin. I was working an eighty-hour week, frantically studying and trying to be a party animal. Something was bound to give. In addition, I felt under massive pressure at the hospital, like most junior doctors do. You don't get rewarded or praised for what you do right; you just get lifted out of it when you get something wrong. The long hours, the sudden and consistent over-exposure to pain and suffering, the huge responsibilities that you can be given prematurely, the lack of sleep, and the general stress of the environment all take their toll. On top of this, I had developed a fairly serious drug habit in order to avoid getting chucked out for my basic lack of intelligence.

I was addicted now, at twenty-five years of age, but I was functioning. I never did drugs at work, just at night in my flat by myself. The social aspect of things had gone by the wayside after the first couple of weeks in this new job. It was all I could do to get through my shift and cram in a bit of study. I don't think anyone at the hospital suspected anything was awry; they didn't really know me and I was very diligent about turning up on time and things like that. The only time I'd have ever given myself away would have been when I sometimes snapped at my colleagues at work or I burst into tears, which would be very out of character for me. But I'd manage to explain it away as being down to lack of sleep and stress. The people around me were happy to believe these excuses; society's denial greatly facilitates the drug addict.

Despite being stupid enough to find myself addicted, at least I was smart enough to know I had a problem. I had only ever wanted to be a doctor, ever since Santa brought me a plastic yellow stethoscope, and I knew I would blow it if I continued as I was. I knew I needed help. No amount of study or hard work was going to get me out of this one. And yet, what stopped me actually seeking help as soon as I accepted that I needed it, was fear and crippling embarrassment because I was a doctor. I muddled through to the end of those first six months of work, and then took two months leave—'for personal reasons'—and threw myself at the mercy of the Rutland Centre. I was a twenty-six-year-old doctor and yet I was terrified, like a schoolchild, the day I was admitted.

Now I see that doctors are exactly the people who would fall into drug use. We're under a lot of stress and we are never taught to take care of ourselves, particularly in that first very difficult year. Everything is so focused on the physical that any emotional and psychological needs of young graduates aren't considered or mentioned. There isn't the time.

———

Emma McCarthy is a thirty-six-year-old nurse in a hospital in Dublin. She was addicted to cocaine and other drugs for a period of thirteen months. She hit a wall when her husband said he was leaving her because her drug-taking was out of control. He threatened to report her at work because she was lying to him, neglecting their young daughter, and possibly endangering her patients.

I think I knew I was an addict before my husband said he was leaving and taking our daughter. But I felt there was nowhere to go. At work, the 'solutions' for staff who presented with personal difficulties seemed punitive, which made me resolve to hide my problem more and to never ask for help.

I had been a model child, teenager, student and then a responsible adult. I rarely drank and hardly went out. I was nearly thirty-three, a married mother-of-one, and a well-liked registered nurse in an obstetrics ward when I first tried cocaine. It was at a staff dinner party actually, and I loved it. It was the best experience I had ever had. Within weeks, I was using it every weekend. I never considered that I might become addicted. I was a nurse, for God's sake. My husband took it the odd time with me but he never craved it the way I did. He never got excited by the prospect of having it that evening, like I would.

. Within about seven months, I was obsessed. I needed it and I was spending all of my spare money on it. I had started doing it alone and in secret. When I couldn't always manage to get away to buy it, I began stealing drugs from the hospital to substitute for it. I had access to the keys to the meds trolley so it was easy. There was an unending supply of painkillers, and when I was signing out drugs like pethidine and morphine for patients, I would make sure to sign for extra and use it myself. They eased the terrible come-down from the coke.

I was functioning fine. My mind wasn't on my job, of course. I was always watching, thinking, plotting. But I think I appeared normal. There would regularly be emergencies with women in labour, but I got by, even though I might have been coked up to the hilt. I don't think other nurses or medical staff knew I had a prob-lem. Certainly nobody ever said anything.

About a year and a half after that very first line of coke in a restau-rant in Rathgar, I came home from work one evening and my husband gave me an ultimatum. I could commit myself to a treat-ment programme or lose my family that very day. I took leave from work and went into the Rutland the following month.

I'm clean nearly twenty months now and I work in the same hos-pital with the same colleagues. Nobody there ever knew and I won't be telling them. I still have days where I crave coke or I imag-ine the morphine in my veins, but I don't give in to it. I hope one day to live without those thoughts.

———

The Sick Doctors Scheme' was founded in 1985 to meet the needs of practising doctors in this country with substance abuse problems. It gives financial and practical help to enable addicted doctors actively in practice to get treatment in special units by specialists in the field. There is also an ongoing programme of

education for doctors about the hazards of substance abuse and the sources of help available. Anonymity and absolute confidentiality are protected above all things.

> 'Doctors from all disciplines, and indeed nurses, have great access to drugs, and this availability certainly puts temptation in their way. All doctors who have or previously have had difficulty with drugs would be loathe to talk about it. They don't like to be reminded of it. The chances of people in the medical profession speaking to you about their use are nil. They guard their profession and their substance abuse with their lives.'
>
> DR AIDEN MEADE, CHAIRMAN OF THE SICK DOCTORS SCHEME

Chapter 3
Money, Money, Money

*Q: How many coke heads does it take to change a
light bulb?
A: More, more, more, more . . .!*

*'I still wish I had more money and my career was
brilliant. All my money went on drugs. But money
doesn't come with instructions and I probably would
have spent it on something else.'*
ALAN, COMPOSER

———

**Forty-eight-year-old events coordinator Marian is a former bou-
tique owner. For the last six years she has been running her own
business organising social events, from black-tie balls and race
meetings for corporate clients, to lunches and gala auctions for
charitable organisations. She has been a recreational cocaine
user for 'at least a decade'. When she set up her own business in
2000 her drug use rose dramatically.**

I used to get through my events in a coke-fuelled haze, snorting up to a gram in an evening. If I had two events in a weekend—which would often be the case during the busy summer season—I would just keep going from the Friday morning until the Sunday night, or Monday morning, without sleep. Coke allowed me to do that. I'd get into Brown Thomas and have my make-up done and pop around to Cats for a blow-dry on the Saturday, do some coke in the car, and then I'd be straight back to the venue.

The stress can be extraordinary and the amount of detail to over-see: guest lists, seating plans, catering, flowers, ice sculptures and a multitude of other things you can't even imagine; so much can go wrong. I used to collapse into bed on the Monday afternoon and wake up sometime on Tuesday in a terrible state, coming down from possibly three bags of coke. But my work was done, and done well.

Now, Marian just uses cocaine as she did 'in the old days'—recreationally, with friends and colleagues—but not at her own events. That's not to say that cocaine doesn't still have a big role to play in her business any more.

Far from it, I reap the benefits of it all of the time. Money is thrown around far more freely when there's cocaine in the house. Everything benefits. Champagne consumption, for example, goes through the roof. Charity balls, in particular, owe a substantial amount of their funds raised on the night to the white lady. Let's just say that if the guests at an auction have been in and out to the loo a lot over the course of the evening it will be reflected in the bids. Cocaine ups the ante more than any amount of photos or figures about hospital equipment. It removes all good sense and charitable intent. It gives rise to displays of wealth and affluence, and people can get fiercely competitive about being seen to have the most, to be the most generous, and of course, at being the centre of attention in a room full of movers and shakers.

I've done it myself, got caught up in the moment and bid out-rageously—and more than I could afford—on things I don't want. And not because I was thinking of the charity. It's such a rush at the time. Money's no object for you and you want everyone there to know that. I've woken up the following day sick as a parrot and down several grand with nothing but a bloody signed rugby jersey in a frame to show for it.

———

'If I even read about coke in the Evening Herald *it'd start me off. I'd get over-excited. I'd be licking specks up off the floor. I would be on the phone and in minutes a guy on a motorbike would be outside with a bag.'*

When we meet in the Westin Hotel, there is something vaguely frayed about Alan. This is perhaps the only indication that he has a story to tell. Well turned out, but with a slightly nervous and worried demeanour, he admits to spending much of his life feeling sorry for himself and divulges the fact that he feels 'much like the character Clov in the opening lines of Beckett's *Endgame***: "No-one suffers like we do." ' He abused speed, pills, cocaine and anything else for many years, despite being in a rela-tionship with a woman who had 'zero tolerance' for drugs. He is forty years old and a composer.**

I was sent to boarding school when I was ten and my mother went away to work in southeast Asia. I was educated at a privately run 'alternative' school. I skipped a couple of years in school, so I was younger than everyone else. I brooded a lot in school, I grew up in the 1970s with separated parents, which was a bit weird back then, so I felt a bit strange. On my first day, I had long hair and wore clogs like the rest of them. I was quite extrovert, but I think I was an object of ridicule really. I remember being taken down to the local barbershop by the headmaster and getting my hair shaved off on the second day.

My mum remarried in my teenage years and I didn't really get on with her husband, but I think most people's teenage years are pretty miserable. Mum paid for my education because I think she was afraid I would turn out mad if I went to a comprehensive, or that maybe I'd start sniffing glue; whereas I actually did that later.

I went to Trinity College to read English. I drank a lot of coffee, smoked a lot of joints, and enjoyed a lot of Fürstenberg. I actually felt though—and I'm sincere about this—I felt I was very under-developed emotionally. I don't know if you know the feeling of doing a language exam, French or Spanish or Italian or something, and you haven't actually learned the conjugation of the verbs, so you're winging it in the exam. That's what I felt I was doing a lot of the time . . . in life. Winging it. And acting the maggot.

I went to the US when I finished in Trinity and had a whale of a time. A year later I was back in Dublin living with my dad and it was fucking depressing to be back. That whole rave scene was starting off then, about 1991, so my friend and I started making music demos and got a record deal. We started making records, writing tunes, programming music and getting paid, then going out to clubs and taking ecstasy.

So the rave scene started to pay but it was a rough place to be— not somewhere I was used to. I was very green about 'how to behave' and I was incredibly fearful as well. I got hospitalised, I got beaten up, my nose was broken; it was quite working class, a tough scene.

The night I did acid for the first time, it blew my mind. I thought, 'Jesus, I've been wasting my fucking time. Why didn't somebody tell me about this before?' I was all ready to do the Jim Morrison bit with the acid so I turned into a bit of an acid–ecstasy head. Within weeks I was heading off on my own having a few extra pills, walking around town by myself. I had a real fear of being middle class and in the kind of clubs where I thought I was going to get fucking thumped so I was feeling uncomfortable and looking over my shoulder all the time.

I started putting a Dublin accent on and changing how I looked, so I'd get away with it—you know, fit in. It was a complicated enough way to be spending your evenings. Originally I thought it was some kind of intellectual experiment I was doing, but I just ended up being totally introspective and then everything became very dark and dismal.

I didn't get into heroin, thank god. In the early 1980s whenever they showed us videos at school, heroin was the only drug mentioned and they would show somebody injecting themselves down at Dún Laoghaire pier or something, and then they would show us a macabre clip of one of the grim treatment rooms in Jervis Street Hospital.

My previous intentions of winning the Pulitzer Prize and getting a few Grammys had gone by the wayside now. I started doing music for ads and I made a lot of money.

I have to say I was a binge user so I'd binge like a maniac on drugs, but then I also binged on sobriety. I'd binge on getting fit for two weeks, come off the cigarettes, swim a couple of miles every day, run and cycle, but it was always pulling the spring back, because then I would let go and be equally extreme on the drug thing. I'd be drugged up to the eyeballs constantly for the following fortnight.

This sounds like I'm some sort of sad old woman on the back of the bus to Knock, but I was actually quite a jovial person, an outgoing person, and I suppose I started getting into coke then because I wanted to know what the fuck all the fuss was about.

The coke scene was different; different people, different places, you know. Some glamour—well, compared to the other gear—

'famous' people backstage at the big gigs, as opposed to being down a lane with the Vicks Vaporub.

Then I got sick, a week after my thirty-fifth birthday. I was diagnosed with a brain tumour and I had to go into hospital for brain surgery. That really frightened me. After my operation, I was getting quite a lot of morphine, which felt great. For weeks or maybe even months after I left the hospital, I used to take 'morphine naps'—morphine sulphate tablets—every morning when I got up, just out of habit. Not for any pain.

I was doing the advertising and music for commercials full-time now and I was making really good money. Composing music for ads and making excellent money. But it was lumpy money; a cheque for £15,000 on a morning and then lots of time off during the day to loaf around. The perfect combination for doing drugs. I filled the free times doing drugs in my working studio, which was on Baggot Street. I would buy champagne and a bag of coke for myself on a Wednesday morning and mix records for the afternoon. I was living in Monkstown and my brother would pick me up to drop me home on his way past at 7 p.m. and I'd have done an eight-ball on my own and had a couple of bottles of champagne. It was a fucking awful life; it's really depressing to recall it now.

I've got epilepsy as a result of the surgery to my brain, so when I was taking all the drugs I used to think, 'I'm going to give myself a seizure here'. It does make you shake a bit. So I started over-using my anti-convulsive medication too. I wasn't to be deterred.

Cocaine is a terrible and dreadful drug. Once you take one line you are on the merry-go-round. It's the old hamster's wheel and the loop gets smaller all the time. You take a line every twenty minutes, then it's every fifteen, then it's every ten, then five, and in no time you don't even bother chopping it anymore.

I obsessed about cocaine. I would be obsessing about it the way you would obsess about a kind of infatuation, like a love affair or something, like your ideal woman. Even if I read about coke in the *Evening Herald* I would get excited. I'd be licking up specks off the floor and stuff like that. I was obsessed and once the obsession got going, I would be on the phone and within minutes I'd have scored. A guy on a motorbike would be outside on Baggot Street with a bag.

Drug dealers have a lot of power; you give all your power away to them. It's like the girl who doesn't want to go out with you, the one you are crazy about. I'd feel the same kind of rejection if I couldn't get my hands on coke quickly enough.

If I met somebody new for business or through friends, I'd actually be really disappointed if they didn't do drugs. But then I also had the business of living and a career to deal with, paying bills and all that. I was still getting the £15,000-gigs very regularly and keeping up my mortgage payments and renting my studio place as well. So it all looked good from the outside. But my only real interest was doing drugs. I became what the people around me justified themselves with: 'At least I'm not as bad as him . . .'

Drugs were always the icing on the cake, so if I wasn't getting any contracts, it'd be: 'Poor me, I better pick myself up with some coke.' If I got a big contract: 'Well, let's celebrate with some coke.'

I suppose I had delusions of grandeur. What can I say? Some people are into equestrian sports, some people like golf—that's their passion. Cocaine was mine. I used to read about it, about its chemical structure and about processing it. I was very well up. I was mesmerised by it. And then of course, I scored, and it was never as good as I wanted it to be and that would be a disappointment. So I'd score again and it'd be one disappointment after another. But the passion remained, and grew.

I compromised my sexuality a good number of times, among predatory gay dealers. When demand was high, your money wouldn't be enough. I was prepared to go that bit further to stay in favour with dealers. To ensure myself a slot near the top of the queue. So that's not a great situation. And it didn't make me feel very good about myself. But I was utterly obsessed with the drug and if this got me some, then I'd do it. After a while, I couldn't look people in the eye, because I felt so shit about myself. I suppose in some really fucked-up way I was thinking, 'Ah you know, all those people going to Reynards are doing it and they are quite successful, so if I do it, maybe I'll be too.' Absolutely pathetic for a thirty-seven-year-old, I know.

At this stage I had a new girlfriend and she had no time for drugs and she could see that they had a grip on me. She got very jealous of that grip and it made her feel very insecure. It was as though I had a mistress. It was like I was obsessing about some other woman.

I'd get phone calls from dealers—I knew a little bit about how the operation worked at this stage—and I just couldn't help myself even though I knew she had a zero tolerance policy. It was a constant battle because I had to hide it from her. I was snorting coke directly out of the bag in the kitchen and thinking she wouldn't know. I mean, it was obvious; I was shampooing the carpet at 5 a.m. listening to techno music.

So she just walked out on me and that was a bit of a shock. All during this time, these years, I had been secretly disgusted with myself. I used to write contracts with myself in the morning at home vowing never to do it again. I'd seal them with wax and I'd post them to myself, but they weren't worth the paper they were written on.

I was doing fucking off-the-wall things, like I would have to present a show reel and I wouldn't have slept for two days. I would shave, cut myself, not shower, put my least crumpled suit on, and go in thinking I was getting away with it. And you always meet your mother's best friend on the DART on those days.

The benders just kept happening and a week bender turned into a twenty-two-day bender and I was getting really out of control now. My brother was asking me not to call into his house, because I was freaking his kids out. I walked around bars on my own. I remember I ended upon on Sandymount Strand in the middle of the night. I was miserable. I was walking by the place my now ex-girlfriend had moved into; she wasn't talking to me. At 5 a.m. walking around, couldn't sleep, all wired, I had run out of drugs. I'd taken some anti-convulsant pills, and I somehow ended up on the strand and I realised 'I'm fucked.'

I rang my brother who picked me up and I vomited all over his car. He put me on the sofa and made me a cup of tea and I've been clean ever since. I think I'd had enough pain. I really had to put my hand in the fire a lot of times before I learned. Some people are better at learning things, but I am not one of life's fast learners. I had to really suffer, and suffer again, and again, before I got the message.

I went into a residential programme in Rutland. After that, I went to my first Narcotics Anonymous meeting in Abbey Street. I thought I'd get mugged. I imagined they'd all be wearing fucking tracksuits. And they were. I'm not one of these guys. Once again I felt like an outsider. It was a familiar feeling of superiority; I've got a fucking degree. I thought they were all losers and there was nobody pretty to look at. But one thing I had to concede was that the people who had been there a while seemed to have something very attractive; they seemed to have a kind of ease with themselves.

I have to emphasise that the Narcotics Anonymous and the whole Rutland Centre thing—I went there for all the wrong reasons. I went there only to get my girlfriend back. But then I stayed for the right reasons, and the right reasons were that my life got better and I got a bit of clarity.

Once you stop using drugs, getting through your first days, first weeks, and your first weekends is very, very difficult. It's a really hard ritual to break. The grooves are cut deep. It's hard to get out of that. Suddenly this really attractive and glamorous thing is gone from your life.

The one thing I would say about keeping off drugs is that it's the first consistent thing I've done in my life. I'm just really getting ambitions and dreams together again and it's coming up to a year now since I used drugs.

For years, my life wasn't about people; it was about, 'Oh, I'll go to that wedding or to that party so I can score,' and I would be in the toilet most of the time. I'm well acquainted with most of the toilets in Dublin City. I still have the obsessive thing. I still go into toilets and think, 'Oh that's a good service.' I notice the shiny, flat surface on the cistern—good for chopping lines.

I still wish I had more money and my career was brilliant. All my money went on drugs. But money doesn't come with instructions and I probably would have spent it on something else. I spent years changing my accent, you know. At least I've stopped doing that.

Anyway, I got the girl and that was brilliant. It was great because I got the feeling that I had a second chance to do things and to be responsible.

I miss the madness sometimes, to be honest with you. But I keep rocking on and doing this for the foreseeable future. I thought I'd have been on my fourth novel by now, collecting a Grammy and meeting Bono for lunch in Dalkey. I'm learning to be a bit more realistic. I did the music for five big TV ad campaigns last year, which was okay.

When I first went to meetings, I used to talk about my brain tumour because I thought I had to say something hardcore to impress the tracksuits, you know. They'd be talking about jumping over counters with shotguns, but I could shock the room too. Beat that, lads.

Chapter 4
Our Pillars

'I started taking a well-known brand of over-the-counter painkillers—Nurofen Plus—for relief from migraines that I had been getting very often. And they worked. I had no headaches and I felt calmer; in fact, I felt great; they gave me a little buzz. I can't really pinpoint when it became a dependency. I just know that within a period of months, I couldn't go a day, a morning, without them. I was driving to chemists in towns far outside the parish to buy a couple of boxes of twenty-four, rather than go into the local place where I was well known. I'd keep track of the chemists I'd been to, and I'd be sure not to go back until some time had elapsed. There were empty boxes in my car, in every drawer in the house. I was a codeine addict, not that I knew it. But I did know that I had a problem.'

FR B., PARISH PRIEST, MIDLANDS DIOCESE

'Yes, I do take drugs—just coke though—regularly enough. I'm certainly not the only one around here that does. The hypocrisy that surrounds it really galls me. *We all know how widespread it is, in bars, offices and over there* [motioning across the road to the Dáil], *but we pretend to be horrified when we read the figures in the papers or hear about rampant use among professionals.*

'When I was a kid, my parents would have people back to the house after church on Sunday mornings. They would all drink fairly heavily into the afternoon. I think at least half of the people they went to Mass with were probably alcoholics. The kids would be left unfed and got up to all manner of mischief while their parents turned into messy drunks in front of them. Then they'd all drive home. You can't tell me that that's any better than adults having a few lines on a Thursday night after work.'

GOVERNMENT MINISTER, BUSWELLS HOTEL,
OCTOBER 2006

———

'I'd go and wait for my dealer in a pub each day. A different pub each day. A good portion of my working week was spent sitting in empty pubs drinking lemonade and watching the door. And he often wouldn't turn up. Or he'd turn up to tell me he'd nothing for me. So I'd have to frantically try somewhere else. Or be physically sick with withdrawals until the next day. If I was an employee, I'd have been fired in no time.'

Rory is a successful businessman. He is very accomplished and well known in advertising, with many high-profile clients. Always a high-functioning workaholic and perfectionist, he was a heroin addict for seven years.

I started using heroin when I was thirty. It just felt so good. I'm not stupid. If it had been awful the first time, I would never have taken it again. The consequences were either far in the future or still only possibilities. By the time some of the real consequences started to impact on me, I couldn't stop so I just had to put up with them. I found it absolutely impossible to stop. I'd do it until I ran out of it. I used heroin on a daily basis—smoking it and injecting it—for a long time.

People would have known I was an addict, but it can be easier to ignore the elephant in the parlour than to point at it. I was working for myself and working in an artistic field, which meant that I could excuse a lot or at least get by without being confronted. There was room for what might have been perceived as eccentricity. Sometimes I worked seven to eleven, sometimes I didn't show up at all. None of the people I worked with would have admitted to knowing that I used heroin, even though I was going out to bars at night with sunglasses on so they wouldn't see my eyes—that kind of shit.

Of course a lot of my colleagues also used, and still use, the same drugs that I did and wouldn't have seen anything wrong with it. Different people ascribe different moral values to different drugs, which I think is a reflection of what people are prepared to do in order to get their hands on those drugs when they become addicted to them.

I used pretty much everything. Anything I could get. Some appealed to me more than others. I was never a big fan of tranquillisers. Speedballs—coke and heroin as a combination—were my favourite. One is a sedative and one is a stimulant, so they hit all your centres at the same time and it's utterly overwhelming.

I was making a lot of money, and an awful lot of it went on drugs. Making all of this money and not paying any income tax, not paying any of my bills. As a result, I'll be paying for my drugs for the foreseeable future because of the backlog of debt that I've amassed.

I was aware of the debts mounting up at the time but everything was far less of a priority than getting the next hit. Once I'd get that hit, I'd have a window in my day in which to worry about bills and work and commitments, but then the hit would wear off and I'd be back to worrying about getting the next one. It's a total preoccupation; very cyclical and very predictable and it's very boring actually. It's extraordinarily boring to get the same narrow range of experiences and feelings over and over again. 'Where am I going to get my drugs?' Then getting them, taking them, being stoned for a couple of minutes, then thinking, 'I really have to knock this on the head' and then back to, 'Where am I going to get my drugs?'

I was living with another addict and she was also strung out. The two of us living together made it about twenty times harder to ever get clean because if either one of us just had a little blip in our resolve, the pair of us would be out the door and using. I only had two relationships with anyone during those years; one with this girl and one with my dealer. Everybody else was just furniture.

We lived in a beautiful house that I'd bought a few years previously in Sandymount and, despite the electricity bills not getting paid and the fridge being empty, it didn't look like a scene from *Trainspotting* or anything. I functioned fairly normally from day to day—once I had my drugs. The degradation and the despair of that time was more internal than external with me. I didn't find myself in horrible dodgy places consorting with geezer types. The surroundings and transactions were always very civil. My dealers were nice guys, with backgrounds similar to my own.

When my dealer eventually got busted, he was held up as an example of absolute cunning—a kind of desperate cunning—because he was one of the first dealers here who was caught successfully using a pager system. This of course meant that, once he was caught, we were all caught because all our phone numbers were in the pager. I remember being contacted by the Gardaí and claiming that he was my plumber!

I placed a huge amount of importance on my work and that probably kept me away from some of the particular pitfalls that I might otherwise have fallen into. The level of interest I had in my work—sometimes I see a similar thing in some female addicts I know, where their thing is their children—that level of interest in something solid might just keep your head somewhat above water.

When I look back at the work I did then, it wasn't bad at all. When I was good I was very good, and when I was bad I was mediocre. I was always very successful in my work. When I was addicted to drugs, I had a particularly low estimation of myself and my abilities and qualities, so I always thought I was really crap. But I was surrounded by people who thought my work was fantastic. It was only much later, when I was in recovery, that I realised they were right!

My reputation was certainly adversely affected by my drug use but not widely enough to have a huge impact. There would've been certain people who may not have booked me for contracts because they knew I was a bit of a drug monster. But still I managed to secure large clients and to complete big projects. I suppose the eventual turning point for me was when I came under a lot of family pressure, particularly from my mother. I was breaking her heart and I knew it. She refused to get off my back. I wanted to get clean myself, so I suppose she provided the push I needed to get the ball rolling. I agreed to go to an NA meeting—just for a look.

One meeting became five NA meetings in a week. I think I became addicted to the meetings. For years, I'd been completely immersed in a drug haze and I'd had the edges knocked off me emotionally. And then I went into these meetings and there were people sitting there who were just the same. I could sense it. I could smell it. I just knew that these people were like me. And they were speaking about things that I'd literally thought, 'I'm the only person who's ever thought or felt these things.'

I know now that my using buddies were all probably feeling

exactly the same things as I was, but you would never admit in a million years to them that you were a bit fucked up about something because if you became the vulnerable one you'd became the object of ridicule and scorn. The whole dynamic of the group was to be better than somebody else and you weren't going to elect yourself to be the one that everyone else felt superior to.

My main dealer for a long time was one of the first people I met when I went to NA meetings. It was quite remarkable. I thought, 'Jesus, if that fucker can get clean then anybody can.'

Drug addicts might have completely different life experiences; one might end up in a Turkish prison and one in a kitchen in Foxrock, but their emotional responses to those experiences are very narrow. When you're using, you've a very small range of experiences, and while they do run deep, they're not very broad.

Everyone's pretending they're absolutely fine, fine, fine, fine. And then you come into meetings and the relief is tremendous. And that's allied with the relief of seeing that these people who are just like you, and who were just as messed up on drugs as you, could get clean and stay clean and end up being reasonably happy.

I did feel the need to change a lot of things right from the start in order to give myself a chance of staying clean and that meant not going and drinking Fanta with all my old friends. If I did, I might have been sipping Fanta but I'd have had a needle in my arm too. I'm not somebody who has a gigantic amount of discipline or willpower, even now.

The second step in NA says, 'We believe that a power greater than ourselves will restore us to sanity' and that set off alarm bells when I first stopped using drugs. I remember talking to another guy at NA and saying, in all seriousness, 'I work in this creative profession. I have to be nuts in order to do my job properly. I don't want to be restored to sanity.' He just laughed at me and said, 'Don't worry. No matter how hard you try, you're going to be nuts for a long time to come.' I took comfort in that.

Drugs made me a part of a lifestyle and a subculture. I felt a lot of pleasure as an addict. But I've achieved some amazing things since I've got clean, some beyond my wildest dreams. I know if I was still using, and still alive, I'd be in a pub poking some unfortunate fucker in the chest with my index finger saying, 'Do you know what I'm going to do some day?' And I would never have done any of it.

——

It's been a big weekend for Seán. His football team won a major trophy on Sunday. His photo, holding aloft the cup they were presented with, is in the local newspaper. A consistent A-student throughout his education, Seán has recently completed his professional exams with top marks across the board. Despite getting offers from the largest and most prestigious firms in Dublin, he is now making his career in his home town. He is the captain of the town's GAA Senior Football team and is in a long-term relationship with a young woman.

I snorted three lines of coke in the locker room before that game. With four of the other guys in that picture. I won't speak for them, but I use coke before almost every game and also three nights a week, on average. And I'm never alone doing it. It makes me feel stronger, more competitive.

I tried it first on a weekend out with some of the boys in Dublin about four years ago. I loved it. I had never really come across it down home before, but once I started looking for it, it was very easy to get my hands on it. It's everywhere now.

Coke is definitely the drug I like the most, but sometimes I'll get in a bag of pills—200 or so—and I'll share them out among my mates. I wouldn't say I 'deal', but I do take in a fair bit above what

I pay for them. If we're having a big night out or someone's having a party, a dozen of us will go through the 200 over that night and morning, no problem. And I'll have a few bob in my pocket at the end of it.

———

When we meet in Avoca Handweavers, it strikes me that Aoife is every inch the schoolteacher. Having arrived early, she has chosen seats at the window, made notes about her story, and has ordered tea for two. Organised and efficient, there is nothing in Aoife's mannerisms to indicate that she is a recovering drug addict.

Born in China to an Irish father and Chinese mother, when she finished school she moved to Ireland alone to attend teacher-training college. At thirty-one, she fell in love with a young professional who was a drug abuser. Not long after, she too developed a drug problem. She lived a double life for a period of three years. She was at once a Head of Department and a drug addict. She managed to maintain the façade and finally got clean in 2003. To this day, her mother and family, colleagues and students, do not know that she is a recovering addict. She teaches in a secondary school in south Leinster.

I was born and grew up in China, the eldest girl of a man from Roscommon and a Chinese woman. I moved to Ireland by myself, when I was eighteen. I was the eldest child and my father had left when I was very young so I never really knew him. So from age five until eighteen, I was raised in my extended family in a very basic and remote part of China. My family life was quite turbulent, with a lot of shouting and so many people in the home but, for the most part, my memories are happy ones and I knew that I was loved by my mother, my brothers, and my mother's huge family.

So I moved to Ireland, which was very liberating for me. I left behind the Chinese culture with all of its restrictions and limitations for women and the big traditional family, and I arrived here ready for my new life. It was a great relief. I could flourish, which meant that I could go to college and work hard by day, and then I could go out all night and live the exciting 'underground' existence that I had long imagined in my head. This was the story of my life. I always had two very different lives running parallel. I was a very good student and a good girl, and then I had this other life, this 'night' life, another life where I was a different person, a different Aoife. I have never had my two selves in synch.

I was a top student with little effort. I had always got A's in school and then in teacher training college. I came here with all of the qualities to live a good and successful life. I was bright and optimistic and full of enthusiasm and zeal, but there was another part of me that really liked spending time with losers. A part of me felt comfortable and at ease with people who had no expectations and no ambitions. So here I was, hanging around with hoodlums and drinkers, people with big problems, people much older than I was. I started drinking quite heavily and smoking dope, but nothing that got out of hand.

I travelled for a number of years and then came back to Ireland, with renewed ambition, the experience of several jobs behind me and ready to teach—a healthy twenty-six-year-old determined to settle and make something of my life. I began teaching in a large, private secondary school on the outskirts of Dublin, and within five years I had established myself within the school and was a Head of Department.

So then I met a great man, Ian, a handsome, recently qualified professional. And he was a drug user. We were both thirty-one. Being the good girl that I was, I tried not to use drugs and I tried to stop him from using, even though he was too far gone down that road for me to help him. He was a cocaine addict and had been for the previous four years. Eventually, I used cocaine with him because if he could not stop, then I would have to take up the habit. I was mad about him and wanted to share his life. All of it.

Looking back I see that I have paid a great price for having him in my life and for loving him, but I would not do it differently. He was too important to my life, and love was very important to me. And feeling at home, which I did with him, was very important to me. It was something I had never fully felt until I met him. So I grabbed onto it at any cost. When I started using drugs with him, it was the first time in my life that I felt that I belonged. And I would do anything for that sense of belonging. I would give my life.

Over the using years that followed, there was always some guilt in me saying, 'What are you doing? How did you end up here? How come you're here in Dublin doing drugs in a house that needs painting and has no curtains? You're a respected teacher. A responsible adult. You mould young minds. What are you doing to your own mind?' I could live my life quite well. I could organise my week and I could get by at work and I could be a model girlfriend to this man. But I couldn't mind my house or pay my bills on time; there wasn't enough of me to go round.

I came from a family with principles; people who lived a good, honest life. There was always a lot of rules and integrity. And I thought that there were things I would never do in my life. I'd never cheat on people, I'd never lie and I'd never steal. And as time went by, I started doing all of those things: cheating people, taking money, manipulating friends, lying all of the time. I was very good at hiding and being deceitful. I think I got to a stage where I was actually devastated by my using. It hurt me, it hurt my heart to be in these awful situations, but there was nowhere else to go. So I stayed in this place.

Time went by, and I was looking at my boyfriend whom I loved very much, and I knew that he loved me. We were both thirty-three-year-old cocaine addicts, living this bizarre double existence. He was a solicitor in a city centre firm, but even I could see that the strain of being a secret addict was starting to show and his health wasn't great. I was a teacher in a highly regarded secondary school. I can see now that I was a completely ineffective teacher, using cocaine steadily every morning in the car park and then at lunchtime or if I ever had an extended free period. But I was never confronted by either the school's management or my colleagues. Perhaps they didn't notice, but maybe some of the students did. I taught Leaving Cert students, some of whom were surely wiley enough to know that I wasn't entirely there.

I remember going to work, the students coming in, and classes changing. I remember doing lesson plans of a sort, getting myself organised in advance so I wouldn't have to think too much during the class and I would be able to retain control, but I didn't actually 'teach'. I gave them work sheets and then I would have them swap papers and mark each other. Maybe some of them liked me because I didn't expect too much of them and I didn't get upset about bad results.

Time was passing and I could see that I was stuck in a dead end. I made a decision not to be a woman that would go down, down, down into increasingly bad health. I was absolutely not prepared to be a junkie for the rest of my life. I formulated a plan in my head; I would buy Ian a trip around Europe for his birthday. If he had some time away from his life, he would get well, and I would commit suicide. It was simple.

I didn't want to die, I just wanted to get out of taking drugs and I didn't have a clue that there might be another way. I didn't want my students and my 'day time' friends to know. I couldn't bear to be exposed, but I knew it had to be just a matter of time before the mask slipped, before I made a mistake and my two separate worlds collided.

So I hatched this brilliant plan: he'll get well and I will die. He went off on his trip and—believe it or not—it did happen for him, as I had imagined. He found recovery in France! We had been speaking on the phone a lot, and one day he phoned me and said he couldn't find anyone to use with there and he ended up in recovery in Lille! I was happy about it, in a way. He would now get better and I could go. Leave this life. It sounds so ridiculously dramatic now, but at the time it was entirely reasonable.

So I fixed up my affairs, wrote some letters, and told the school that I would finish at the end of term in June. It was now the end of March. I was very cool about it; I had tried life, and I had failed—I had lost the fight. There was no point in going on about it.

But I think Ian knew there was something amiss, because one day in early May, he came back. Out of the blue. And my plans had to be cancelled, because he was around now and he was beautiful and tanned and healthy and I loved him. But things were very different between us. And not in a good way for me. He was struggling with recovery but feeling very determined, and he looked good and he was attending NA regularly. Meanwhile I was being left behind using cocaine at our kitchen table before work, destroying myself, harbouring thoughts about suicide. He would read the bloody 'Twelve Steps' aloud to me having his coffee! I was very jealous; he had this new interest, this new thing, without me. I got very angry. I heard him on the phone one Friday evening talking to his new NA friends who were advising him to leave me, if I didn't want to get clean.

The next morning I was in bed, depressed and full of self-pity, in a total state, hating him and gripped by the fear that I was losing him—when I picked up his notes and starting reading the Steps. And I decided then to go to the next meeting with him. I think part of me wanted to confront those guys who were telling him to leave me! I was ready for a fight! I got into the room and sat in the chair and of course there wasn't a peep out of me.

It was May 2002 and I was thirty-four years old. It was the last day that I used cocaine. I didn't go back to the school in September.

I wanted time to get myself together and to start again, as the committed teacher I had once been. I started a new position in a school in Wicklow in September 2003.

And in that December, we married—both of us struggling to stay clean and full of fear and hope. That was three years ago. Ours has been a great love affair.

———

'I ate prescription painkillers like Smarties, day and night, for over ten years. I knew it wasn't ideal and I kept them hidden from everyone, but I have to say, in many ways they were what allowed me to live a successful life. I was working away, I got the top employee in my firm, I was bettering myself, doing further exams, flying along. I was certainly functioning—more than functioning; I was an achiever during this time. I got married and was respected in the golf club; life was motoring along nicely. Certainly better than it had been before.'

Niall was made partner in his actuarial firm five years ago. Now forty-one years of age, he came out of a treatment centre for a decade-long addiction to prescription drugs three weeks ago. He is the vice-captain of a golf club and has been married for eleven years.

As a teenager, I was at a lot of parties where there were drugs but I never partook. I had no interest. I might have had the odd drink, but I could take or leave it. I had a lovely family, good upbringing, privileged education. I succeeded academically. I was a happy kid. Nothing that would have earmarked me for what was to come.

Just after I finished secondary school, I went to my dentist who noticed that I had no protective enamel left on my teeth and suggested that I must suffer with stomach acid. This led to an appointment with a consultant who ran tests and discovered that I had a very serious problem with my stomach. I had my first serious operation shortly after—twenty-six others were to follow over the next fifteen years.

That first operation was in the old Adelaide Hospital in Dublin. My first experience of drugs was then. I was on a lot of painkillers and also on a morphine-based drug called Omnipom, which—it transpired—I was allergic to. I was in a coma for three days. I had a lot of problems post-operatively, so I didn't really want to go back to the same surgeon. When I had the same acidic symptoms again two months later I went to a top surgeon in St Vincent's Hospital. He performed the same operation. At this stage, I have to admit, I did enjoy the pain relief but I wasn't addicted to it. That operation didn't work either.

A year or two later, the same doctor performed another operation—a more detailed procedure that he hadn't tried the previous time. The procedure was a success in many ways, but my bowel and stomach did not 'wake up' from the operation. They stayed dormant for a period of over four months so I couldn't eat or drink. I was being fed through tubes, losing weight, confined to bed. At the end of the four months, complications occurred which resulted in another thirteen-hour operation, the result of which was the removal of most of my stomach and a large part of my bowel. I was very ill at this stage and spending extended periods in intensive care. During this time, I was heavily sedated on morphine. I haemorrhaged and had further clearing-out surgery, during which I nearly lost my life.

It was a desperately difficult time. My entire life was on hold—everything. I had no experience of being 'in my 20s'. My friends went to Australia to travel and off to see the world, but those things were never an option for me. I studied and worked for periods between my various spells in hospital. I managed to always maintain my A average in exams. At this point, I had been out of work for six consecutive months due to illness.

My life had to accommodate my 'new' body so I could only eat very small amounts. I was like a newborn baby—the way they cry because they have new and unfamiliar cramps and wind. Just like a baby, I had a new system and my brain had to get used to it.

Mentally, I was suffering a lot too. I had reactive depression, which is still with me today. I went to see an eminent psychiatrist in Dublin who was of the belief that everything could be fixed with a tablet. Before I knew it, I was on eleven different tablets including sleeping pills, Valium, anti-depressants … you name it, I was taking it, and I was more than happy to.

They were so strong that I actually was numbed. I couldn't feel or function emotionally. I was floating through one day into the next. I had qualified as an actuary and I was beginning to achieve in my career, but in many ways I just wasn't there. People who know me well say I was in a permanent daze, a different world. I was just twenty-six at this stage. The doctor had no long-term plan or programme for me. I was to continue taking these pills and live my life this way. He did next to nothing for me by way of psychology or talking therapy. My father would fill my prescriptions for me sometimes and couldn't believe the amount of meds I was taking, but everyone was so used to me being ill and hospitalised that I suppose it all seemed necessary. By now, there was general concern growing among my family about my depression.

One day I was in the office, and I had these terrible cramps and pains and I ended up in the hospital again for a few days. It turned out I had adhesions—like scar tissue or scabs on the inside of my body—which had the effect of blocking everything up, so I had to have surgery again and large amounts of pain relief. Meanwhile, I was still taking the dozen tablets daily, as prescribed by my psychiatrist. I had quite serious surgery at least once a year from then on for adhesions, to maintain me. So the morphine from the hospital and the tranquillisers every day of the week were pretty much constant now, and I was certainly addicted to morphine at this stage. I enjoyed it on two levels—it made me feel better physically, and it took away the doubts and the depression and the sorrow that I lived with. The morphine made me aware of the power of some drugs and the peace to be found within them. I still hated the tranquillisers, however. I knew they were bad news and not helping me at all.

I had recently met my wife-to-be and she was very supportive. She noticed that the pills I was taking for my depression were having little positive effect so we took a decision between us that I would come off them straight away. I didn't want to be taking them in such high doses. She didn't think that my cramps and stomach problems would be helped by my taking all of these other medications, so I came off them. I knew I couldn't continue the way I was; I seemed to be taking more and more things and feeling worse. I experienced horrendous cold turkey for a couple of weeks but after that I saw an immediate effect in terms of my levels of alertness and efficiency. When I told the psychiatrist, he told me that I would fail and that I'd end up back on them. I stopped seeing him after a further year because I certainly wasn't getting better.

I did a stint in St John of God for depression; I was in a really bad way and finding it hard to cope. While I was in there, I was on a fierce high dose of everything. They doubled the dose of Valium for starters, which numbed me to an unbelievable degree. Despite the numbness, I knew when I was there that it wasn't the right place for me. I started to panic about getting out and even falsified not being depressed so that I could leave. I came out of there worse than I went in. I had gone in hoping that they could do something to make me better and all they did was increase my drugs and keep me quiet, that kind of carry-on.

I was in and out of hospital year in and year out when my doctor told me that the operations couldn't continue. My body couldn't take it anymore. He suggested strong pain relief instead so that I could manage my life. What he prescribed were addictive tablets and that's where the trouble really started with my addiction. These were a new venture for me. They gave me a buzz and are hugely addictive and very popular. I know people who are addicted to them now. And I've been addicted to them since then—it was 1994. They got me through the day. I was using them as painkillers—as they were intended—and also as an anti-depressant. The buzz gave me a lift and kept me going. I was off the anti-depressants now and using these painkillers by the bucketload, irrespective of whether or not I was in any pain. I thought this was a far preferable situation. If you had taken them away from me for one day, I'd have had a bad day. In fact, it wouldn't have happened. Because come hell or high water, I'd have found another pharmacist or place to get them.

My wife knew nothing about any of this. She was so proud and pleased for me that I had managed to kick the tranquillisers. That was it, as far as she knew. I was very controlled about guzzling my pills, and once I had them, all was well. Simple really. I'd get a buzz for an hour and then I'd take them again. And then at lunchtime, after lunch, in the evening, a handful in the car before I went into the house, in the bathroom before bed . . . all of the time really. I'd get prescriptions, and I'd falsify prescriptions and I'd copy them and re-use them, go to different pharmacies. I never had any difficulty getting them filled.

I knew I was really addicted and I knew that someday I was going to have to do something to get out of it, but it never seemed to be the right day. I didn't have the courage and I didn't know how to break the cycle. Also, it seemed a terrifying prospect and not one that I wanted to face. I'd been through so much and the idea of going back to the chronic pain again just wasn't inviting.

After a decade or so of lying and forging scripts and popping pills, I deliberately got myself found out. I had reached a stage where I couldn't sleep at night any more, so I started popping sleeping tablets too. Sleeping tablets are not something that you can hide. I would effectively pass out into an unnaturally deep, coma-type sleep shortly after taking them. After a period of this happening every night, and often at different times of the day and during the weekend, Jane knew I was taking something and questioned me. I think her suspicions also alerted her to other anomalies in my behaviour and she started watching me more closely. I admitted what I was doing, the whole lot. I seized the opportunity to get it all off my chest. I thought I could tell her, and she'd help me and everything would be fine. She was horrified, shocked, frightened; I'd been lying to her for ten years and she hadn't spotted it. I was lying, manipulating people, trying to cod myself. I was no different to the junkie on the street who'd do any-thing for his fix. So things didn't improve for me then the way I'd stupidly assumed they would.

I started drinking then too, not a huge amount at all, but mixing alcohol with sleeping tablets and these painkillers is a no-no. I'd black out and pass out. Things were really getting out of control. Four months ago, I tried to stop taking the sleeping tablets and to cut down on the pills and I ended up really very low, having suici-dal thoughts and really it was the bleakest time ever. I binge drank for an entire weekend, which is something I had never done before in my forty-one years. When I came out of that, I knew I needed serious help. Now I was fighting drink, depression and the aware-ness that I had a drug addiction. I needed to go somewhere to get out of the loop, somewhere to dry out a bit before I got myself a place forresidential treatment in the Rutland.

I went back into St John of God just for two weeks. I was more in control of it this time and I didn't allow them to sedate me overly. They put me on a non-addictive tranquilliser and I put on two stone in weight. I was delighted. I'm now up to over eleven stone for the first time in my life. I can't ordinarily put on weight because I have next to no stomach. My self-esteem has really improved because of the extra weight. I have a brother who is only thirteen months younger than me and now, for the first time, we actually resemble each other. I'm not the 'thin one'. It's nice, you know. It feels normal.

I was apprehensive about going to the Rutland. I knew it was a closed centre, with no mobile phones and tough tactics. I was worried that I wouldn't be able for it, to tell you the truth, I wasn't feeling very strong or resilient. I didn't know if I could take being knocked down before being built back up. I'm not discriminating against the people who go there, I have heard wonderful stories about recovery, but I just didn't think it would suit me. I'm not a tough guy! So I decided to check in to Forest—the treatment centre in Wicklow—instead. My wife had phoned them and set up an assessment for me. It was my first time ever in addiction treatment and I checked in for four weeks.

I found their self-motivational programme fantastic. It really worked for me. It's a different way of doing things—lots of long walks and positivity—compared to the other centres in this country, but it works for me. There were a couple of guys there who took advantage of the less-closed nature of things and would come back stinking of drink, but they're fooling themselves. I was determined that it would work for me. The vhi covered it. I have aftercare now with a counsellor once every two weeks. It's only been a few weeks and of course I still have the cravings—every day—but I'm committed to being clean and I have to take one day at a time.

I'm in a difficult position because I still suffer with physical pain and I always will, so I do need pain relief. It's a fact of my life. The tablets that I need to take are addictive by nature. I need to learn control. Now I'm just on a low, recommended dose of Prozac, and my pain relief is monitored by my brother. He keeps my tablets and prescriptions and gives me just the amount that I'm required to take to keep my pain in check.

My wife and I went through a very difficult time and I feel really bad for her. Some people say she's too hard on me, but I think I need someone who will give me a kick in the backside. I'm not into pity parties. There are those who say I've had a tough time; all the operations and scares and no stomach. But that doesn't excuse my addiction. It's nonsense to say that at this stage of my life I can explain away my actions because of poor health. I've lied and hurt a lot of people. I need to bring closure to that whole area of my life and just get on with the rest of it. Things are okay between Jane and me at the moment. She sees that I'm committed to a new leaf and that I'm trying to get and keep control on things.

I do think about filling prescriptions that my brother wouldn't know about—having a separate stash—but I have to put those thoughts out of my head. Jane worries about that and some days she questions me about how much medication I've taken. She doesn't want to take control of my pills. She doesn't want to be responsible for measuring out what I need. She's being honest about it—she feels it's too much for her to take on. We're married eleven years now and the ten years that she didn't know about my addiction were great, but this has been a very difficult year for us as a couple. I blame myself for all of it. Jane didn't ask for this. She didn't know what she was getting. I was lying to her. I brought this problem to the party. I love her to bits and she's been there through thick and thin, although we have been close to separating because of it. Things will surely get better from here on out.

I'm in NA now and I've met some great people there. I go to meetings close to where I live and I don't give a shit if someone recognises me or otherwise. It's there for when I'm having a bad day. Likewise, I can call my therapist at Forest any time I need to. A lot of people in NA worry about me because I'm vice-captain of my golf club and there's a lot of drink around and maybe I'm putting myself 'in harm's way'. But alcohol has never been a problem for me. With the exception of that weekend, I've never had any interest in alcohol.

My deepest wish is that in a year or two I will have established some control over my drug use and that the cravings will be gone. I've got to bring manageability back into my pain relief. And I have to do this myself. I can't ask my brother to measure out my pills for the rest of my life. My goal is to be able to take the amount of painkillers that my condition requires, without becoming addicted to them again. It'll be difficult.

I do feel that during all those years of surgery, I might have benefited if a medical person had spoken to me about the possible emotional or psychological effects that so much serious illness and grave, dangerous operations might have on me. I was a young guy in his teens and twenties.

I'm belting away now at work and keeping busy otherwise with the golf club. I have a couple of dogs and a few horses and I've great plans to live a healthier life. Everyone has been very support-ive. They don't know about the drugs and the addiction but there's an unsaid understanding that I suffer with depression. I don't shy away from the depression thing, but I don't mention the addiction to anyone. The senior partner in my firm knows about the drugs, but otherwise I don't go on about it. As I said, I'm vice-captain now in the club and will be captain in the next couple of years, please God, so I mustn't have ever behaved too badly! They've all been complimenting me over the last few weeks about how well I look since my operation six weeks ago! I wasn't going to say I'd actu-ally been in rehab for a ten-year addiction to prescription drugs.

My parents had a difficult time; they had been feeling sorry for me and pitying me and my lot for so long, and then it transpires I've been lying to their faces and manipulating them for years. They knew I had been taking anti-depressants years ago but they didn't know anything about the forged prescriptions and my addiction. Now it's all in the open and it's a relief.

I have to have a positive attitude now. I've been through the worst and hopefully I won't need any more surgery. I'm glad to see the back of my thirties and it's a new era now. I'm sorry that I ever went to that dentist! My younger brother had the same symptoms and the same condition as me. He had his operation a number of years after mine, by keyhole surgery. He was in and out in thirty minutes.

————

In his mid-thirties, Councillor Flanagan is the Deputy Mayor of Roscommon and a father of two young daughters. A confirmed drug user himself, he was elected to the County Council in Roscommon in 2004.

I find this idea of drug 'pushing' laughable. Pushing? It's far from pushing that drug dealers have to get involved in. Once word spreads that an individual is dealing drugs, he will be plagued by users with money to the point that he'll have to turn them down many times, and switch off his phone. The dealer would need an unending and unlimited supply of the damn things if he was to even think about getting into pushing. Nobody needs to push drugs. It's a pull. The drug trade is based on the economics of pulling, rather than of pushing. Who would be pushing something that there's never enough of?

I've never been much of a fan of class-A drugs myself. I have used cocaine a number of times and ecstasy, but not a lot. Among my friends and colleagues here in Castlerea, I'd be the odd one out when it comes to class-A's. My drug of choice is cannabis. I smoke it five or six days a week, at different times. The one standard in my routine is to smoke at ten o'clock at night when the Vincent Browne show comes on the radio. I've been smoking cannabis at this level for fifteen years or so.

When my grandfather died, my grandmother was perfectly and logically hysterical. She had been married to the man for most of her life and to help her deal with what was very natural grief and hysteria, her doctor gave her tranquillisers. Twenty years later when she was admitted to hospital with a broken hip, she was still unquestioningly taking her tranquillisers every day. The pill use was abruptly stopped in the hospital and my grandmother spent her final days going through the hell of cold turkey. That's the level of understanding that people have of drugs in this country. Something that the GP prescribes for two decades to an elderly and upstanding lady is fine, no matter what it is or why. The reality was that my grandmother was a drug addict for twenty years.

Trying to stop people using drugs by telling them that they're fuelling crime won't work. If you were to ban apple tarts, you would have a black market of the bloody things. People would get them somehow. I'll show you how I'm not fuelling crime; those plants growing there in my back garden are cannabis plants. In about a month's time, I'll move them to the bog and let them grow there. I am, in fact, suppressing crime—in a sense—because I give it away to friends. If you can get a substance at a shop and not have to deal with what you might call low-lifes to get it, then you will go to the shop—even if it's three times the price. To say that people would still go to dealers, with the multitude of risks that that involves, is nonsense.

Illicit drug use is rife among all classes, or else there are a few hundred lower-class people with little money guzzling over a billion euros' worth of drugs with their mates every year. And I think we all know that that's not the case. Do people really believe that massive amounts are being used—enough for fifty people each—by the heads from the likes of Blanchardstown and these places, and that none of the professionals living in Dalkey indulge at all? I find that level of denial, as a society, utterly mind-boggling.

'I need help now. I know that. I've tried to stop using myself but I can't, so I'm starting a treatment programme soon. I have to be clean first, or they won't take me. I'm ready to be. I haven't used anything in nine days.'

SISTER ITA

THE WESTBURY HOTEL, JULY 2006

A petite, wiry lady with short, mousey hair, Sister Ita provides the single biggest moment of shock of all my days researching this book. She appears at the top of the stairs into the hotel's foyer and briskly walks the length of the room, trying to locate me from the colours I've told her I'll be wearing. Spotting me, she stops scanning the faces and gives me a small smile. Although she is coming my way, I still don't stand to greet her. I can't believe this is her. She is wearing her habit.

I've used at least a dozen different drugs over the past two years, but cocaine is my drug of choice. I don't have to pay for it. A gentleman who comes to me to talk and to unburden himself a couple of times a week gives it to me. He introduced me to this world—I knew nothing of it before—when he spoke to me that first time.

I approached him in the church one afternoon because I had seen him there a few times by himself and he looked like he was very troubled, struggling with the weight of something. Over time we have developed a strong friendship. He's a married man, but his children are grown up and he and his wife have drifted apart. He is weak and sees prostitutes from time to time. He can't live with himself and the shame, so he uses drugs. It's a dreadful, vicious cycle and he can't find his way out of it. He talks to me about it all and I listen. About his plans to stop, about the drugs and the girls, and how much he loves his wife. I don't judge him. But now I'm full of guilt and pain for my weakness and my behaviour. I can't look in the mirror, let alone do God's work. I don't know what made me try it—cocaine—that first time. Perhaps it was the chance to experience a thrill, just for a few minutes. And it was a thrill. A great thrill.

I've been a nun for eleven years. It's all I was ever sure of. Now, I don't know who or what I am. I used to think that nuns lived a privileged and lofty existence, somehow protected from life's temptations and horrors. That makes me laugh now. I'm as susceptible to the same things as anyone else and I've failed myself, my Order, my vocation.

God watches us all, even the clergy. And, for my sake, I hope it's true that he forgives and loves us all.

Chapter 5
Silence: the Irish Answer

'Ireland is still the island nation of old. Everybody knows everybody, we love to know each other's business, we're especially keen on hearing about our neighbours' misfortunes. Parochialism is rampant like a disease and that leads to secrets, shame, denial, embarrassment and silence—all those horrible words and feelings.

'Many people use drugs as an anaesthetic, to stop the pain of something. It's often either a sense of isolation or something that they feel is shameful and embarrassing. This can frequently be of a sexual nature. Catholicism and the associated no-no that was, and is, attached to sexual behaviour has sponsored shameful and repressed feelings and thoughts for a long, long time.

'Most addicts I see are very sensitive people and part of their drug abuse is to switch off that sensitivity.'
GERRY HICKEY, PSYCHOTHERAPIST AND COUNSELLOR

———

'No matter where I go or who I see, I see Mammy and Daddy, and Mammy and Daddy see me.'

Peter is in his 50s and a partner in a large and long-established accountancy firm. He was addicted to prescription drugs for a period of almost twenty-four years. He has been in recovery since 2000.

I traded on the same two prescriptions for Valium and sedatives from 1977 until 2000. I had two chemists and, honest to Christ, it was criminal how they filled those prescriptions, year in, year out. I'd have the little card with the code for the medication on it. I made up three or four of those cards and kept them in various places at home. I would always go in wearing a suit and looking very sharp. A problem only ever arose when there was a locum on: 'I can't fill this for you.'

With that, absolute terror would run through me. The arrogant and overbearing side of me would answer: 'I beg your pardon?'

'I can't fill this for you. This prescription is ten years out of date.'

'I had no problem getting my prescriptions filled up the road, and I don't have a lot of time to wait, so what are you going to do?' I was quite, quite good at confrontation.

Some seconds—which seemed like hours—would pass. Beads of sweat would be forming on my brow and my fists would be clenched behind my back to stop me shaking.

'Well, I'll fill it for you this time, but you better go to a doctor and get a new one as soon as you can.'

The relief would start flooding through my body, but still the arrogance: 'Look, I'm not going to make a separate journey to the doctor for it, but the next time I'm with him I'll mention it, if I remember to.'

I would come out then and go to the other chemist and do the same. If I was travelling somewhere I would always have to have at least seventy tablets in my luggage and seventy tablets on me. They would last me for a few days. It was a familiar situation. I was the squirrel with my nuts secretly stashed all over the place. I was never ever without my medication or my prescriptions, because that would be a fate worse than death.

I was hugely judgmental when I first went for help for my addiction. There was a guy talking about having his works hanging out of his ankles. I couldn't believe what I was hearing; him recounting stories of beating people up and robbing them, but I might have done something similar if that locum hadn't filled my prescriptions.

I'm the youngest of four, from a large rural town in the midlands. My mother came from a very well-to-do business background in the town and my father was a civil servant. She never fully accepted him because she was one of 'The People' in the town. Everything that we had had come from her, and she never tired of letting us all know. She was very, very cold and was always very concerned about what other people thought, to an alarming extent. And I bought into it as a little child. My father was a terribly quiet and gentlemanly type of guy and he was the one who showed us love and affection. My mother didn't at all. We had paid staff in the house to do everything and to raise us boys. My mother had very little input into our care.

Our family was part of the institutional thing of the town that we lived in and was very, very close to the Catholic Church. To me now looking back on it, it was Stalinistic and tyrannical. We—my mother particularly—were very highly regarded by the neighbours and by the priests who would visit our house. She was always watching what was going on in the area—that peculiarly Irish thing of keeping up, and doing one better. I remember always being compared with our neighbours and our cousins.

My three older brothers were not achieving academically as much as she would have liked. There was this sense of panic in the house, that she was being let down. Every day she'd point out other people in the town who had far less materially than we had, had far less opportunities, and yet they were doing better. And our cousins! How well they were doing and how badly we were doing. And all this went on inside the home incessantly. So there was this kind of pull, this contradiction that on the one side we were supposed to be part of the upper echelons of this community but on the other side we just weren't good enough to be. We weren't pulling our weight.

I can remember being four or five years of age and being glad to go to bed because of the rows that were going on in the house. I knew that there was something wrong but as I got older I started to accept it, this mayhem and panic. I saw myself as part of the problem and I would actually try to fix things and make them better. I became a 'fixer' at probably seven or eight years of age. It was an awful lot on little shoulders. It's sad now to say it out loud.

I cry now looking at those animal programmes where you see the little animals at play, and part of the play is to equip them for hunting. I see little bears or tigers at that young age playing with their siblings, and it hits me how we never actually had that at all. The relationship between my brothers and myself—while we get on fine together—is poor. We can't talk about things, other than our new cars or houses.

So from about seven, I became an over-achiever and a people pleaser. I wanted to deliver what my mother wanted of me. Of course, the reality was that nothing would have ever pleased her. I was obsessed with doing well, being seen to be doing well, and with looking the part. I bought into her claims about how we hadn't wanted for anything material, but I wasn't aware of the desert and the deficit on the whole emotional side. Life in our home was a constant struggle to maintain the façade that she wanted.

From the age of about nine or ten I developed a massively obsessive thing with masturbation. Sexuality was very distressing to me. I felt I was a freak and the priest coming to the house all the time didn't help, so I ended up then with this huge worry because of the whole religious aspect of it. I remember lying awake at night paralysed with fear as a ten- or eleven-year-old, crying because I'd committed a mortal sin, and knowing that if I died that night I was going to hell.

As a young boy I started going to confession twice a week. We went to Mass on a Sunday, but we were paraded up and down the church and I worried about going to communion in this state of mortal sin, because then I surely was going to die and never get out of hell. The amount of energy that I spent turning hell and sin over in my head, living in fear and panic as a young boy, is astonishing.

I started drinking by myself from about twelve. I was building a wall around myself, hiding from things and feeling shameful and alone, especially the whole masturbatory thing. When you see fireworks going up over Sydney harbour, that's what it was like for me the first time I drank as a little boy.

My mother never drank, my father would have taken a brandy now and then, but there was always drink in the house. Then I started working with a cousin of mine who had an off-licence, so I could take drink from their stores without them knowing. Or if I was short of money, I could get some out of the till.

I went to boarding school during the week and academically I swept the board. I was getting class prizes and all of that. I remember then when there was a presentation of class prizes, my mother turned up but my father didn't, and that was unusual—for him to not be always there for me. But I think he just didn't feel part of all of that show and nonsense. So I was achieving, but running alongside this was a very sad little kid with the beginnings of a serious drinking problem.

I couldn't socialise at thirteen, fourteen or fifteen years of age because I was overwrought and tense. And yet, I became very skilled at keeping up a façade of appearing comfortable—like we did at home. This skill was to help me in my professional career later because I became really very skilled at dealing with people, and dealing with people's problems so long as they weren't my problems, and I became very good in the whole area of mediation.

At thirteen and fourteen I would put away a couple of bottles of whiskey from the stores and maybe a few large bottles of beer. I began stashing it in an area at the back, in a place accessible to me when everything else was closed down. At night I could come back there like a little squirrel accessing his hoard. So whenever I needed drink, I had drink, from a very young age. Alcohol removed me from me. I was free. I'd say from fifteen years of age, I was drinking a naggin of whiskey and two large bottles of beer before I went to the local dance or whatever was on.

When I got old enough to be drinking in a pub, I would always order the first round. Money was never a problem for me. I would get the first drinks and I would buy a large gin, raw without a tonic, to drink while I was waiting for the rest of the order. I would bring another large gin and a pint of beer back to the table for myself. In the local town it was a badge of honour to be able to 'hold your drink'. One's role models in the area were people who could drink maybe seven or eight pints or ten whiskeys and still be able to stand.

As I got older, it was fast becoming obvious that no woman was going to be good enough for my mother to accept as a partner for her youngest son. I had learned from my brothers who had gone before me that anybody they were involved with was never good enough. She advised me about every girl to 'keep away from her', all of this sort of thing. I think there was a kind of anti-women element to it too. Looking back on it now, my mother had very few female friends. She was hugely judgmental; we got seed, breed and generation of that person and how they weren't good enough. What should I have done? Turned and said to her: 'Listen, would you ever piss off with yourself—I want to live my own life.' I wish I had.

I was the person in the family who was pleasing her the most, because I was achieving. The pressure I felt to maintain this sat very heavily on my shoulders. I can't say I had it tough growing up, in so far as I wasn't beaten or abused. The deficit at home was in the area of the expression of love, and I think it happens in a lot of Irish families. We were provided for materially, but never nurtured or praised, and the bar was always being set so high that it was impossible to keep up.

Rarely will you have a situation where there is only one pea in the pod that is injured or bruised, because you are all coming from the same background. One of my other brothers' reaction was to rebel against the whole thing. Now this brother is hugely successful in business but, by Christ I tell you, he has so much anger. He has so much anger in him it is unbelievable. At this stage, he is in his late sixties and he finds it difficult to deal with anything. All three of my brothers have serious addiction issues to this day.

After school, I studied Business and Politics at university and then became apprenticed to a local accountancy and legal firm. I joined local political clubs and became very involved in professional associations in the legal field. Somebody looking on would have said that I had it all together. You can't very easily throw off the conditioning you get. It became more important for me to achieve and to score in these areas of business and wealth than it was to succeed in the fundamentals of actually living—relationships, getting married, having children and all of that.

The higher I got in the local area with regard to my profession, the more satisfied and comfortable I felt. You see, this was satisfying my mother. I had an incredibly debilitating sense or fear of failure. I was getting more and more prominent and becoming very successful, quite quickly. I felt that if I started getting involved in relationships, I might well fail because I wasn't equipped for them. If a relationship failed, it would be a massive black mark against the golden boy I was becoming. Business is more predictable. I could score very highly in areas where success was a case of black or white—easily quantifiable.

I moved to Dublin soon after. I enjoyed it, the people, the scene and I enjoyed the whole social end of things. I became a real social butterfly. Anything that was going on in Dublin, I was there. I would very often get my photograph in the papers at some social gathering, and I craved this type of thing. I was my mother's son then more than ever.

I wanted to buy into everything that she was. I wanted to maintain her world. I wanted to please her and to please people. I remember meeting a guy from the inner city at a Narcotics Anonymous meeting. He was less than half my age with no education at all and he told my story in one line when he said: 'I always tried to be what I thought everybody wanted me to be.'

As I go back and look at my career and my social life, I always did what I thought I should. For example, from my background I loved country and western music, but when I came to live in Dublin I wouldn't let anybody see the tapes because it just wasn't cool to do it. I wouldn't be seen with people that it wasn't cool to be seen with. I was always with the right people in the right places, and to keep that going is a hell of a burden. I felt that that was the only way to live life.

Years later, a counsellor asked me to write down all the things I didn't like about my mother. Then he asked me to put a tick after all of those things that were characteristics that I also have. Christ, it took me three months to get over that.

I gave up drinking when I was twenty-eight because of the whole unmanageability of it in my life, having to drink before work in the mornings, drinking at lunchtime, drinking during the afternoon. A lot of it was work-related because there was a lot of entertaining and it was quite acceptable to drink a bottle of wine and a couple of gin and tonics with lunch.

I remember setting off for Donegal on a Friday morning for a weekend, and I drove the car into a ditch after only two miles. I was very drunk, but I ploughed on and got there by about 10 p.m. I stayed up until 4 a.m. drinking. The next morning things were so bad, I remember going down to the bar in the hotel and not being able to actually lift a gin and tonic in my hands. The guy who owned the hotel took me to the doctor and he gave me a shot of Valium in the backside and then another about five minutes later.

Following that, I had a few escapades abroad of wakening up and not knowing where I was or how I got there. So I went off the drink and instead began to take medication—tranquillisers and sedatives and that sort of thing. I began to credit myself a lot for not drinking but I was immediately addicted to prescription drugs.

So I was not drinking at all now and I appeared to be living normally. I was getting involved in relationships again. I was popping these pills all through the day and night and they stifled the heebie-jeebies that I'd get.

I had rows with my mother at this stage because she used to make unkind references to my father, who had died a little time previously. She scoffed at me because I had respected him even though it was she who had given me everything. I told her that he had given me love. She found it very difficult to hear any criticism. She thought she was the perfect woman.

Fifteen years passed—it was the mid-1990s—and I was living on meds. My career had been flying high but the spark had gone. Definitely. Relationships and work started to suffer. My mental health was breaking down and my confidence was gone to the extent that I couldn't actually leave the house. If I went to the supermarket I would get a panic attack and want to run out. If I wanted to pick up even a loaf of bread I wouldn't go to the local shop. I would go to a supermarket miles away, because if I met somebody I knew I wouldn't be able to deal with it. In the supermarket, even if it was only a pint of milk that I wanted, I would have to bring a trolley with me because that would hold me up if I met somebody. I couldn't go to a restaurant for a meal. I couldn't go to see a film because of this fear of losing control of myself. This fear of being in the cinema and not being able to stop myself shouting out, 'Oh you fucking bastard' or something, in the black quietness.

Now I know that that comes directly from the whole oppressive need to control life. Maintaining control and making sure that everything appears to be fine, but something within you saying,

'Well, I'll show you,' and this lack of control rearing its ugly head. I couldn't trust myself not to jump out of the box and cause chaos.

I knew by now that taking these drugs was a major sign of weakness. I wasn't socialising anymore. On a good day I could get to the supermarket. On a bad day I could only bring myself to watch the television. I was going to work and keeping to myself. The long lunches were unthinkable now. I couldn't have lunch at all actually. I started making up excuses, saying I was going for a swim or something, and then having a bottle of water and a sandwich in my car by myself.

Eventually, I wasn't able to turn in to work at all and I missed a very important meeting. My friend—the managing partner—rang me and I broke down on the phone. I told him about my panic and depression, but not about the drug addiction. My house was beautiful, in a nice leafy suburb, but I was under house arrest. And the inside of it was going to pot.

I went to my doctor and I told him the full story, and he shook his head. He told me I would always be on some medication because it's not possible to be on drugs for that length of time and just stop. He started throwing out disheartening statistics: something like only 10 per cent of people who are on prescription drugs ever try to come off them and only 1 per cent of that 10 per cent will ever be successful. He told me that my body would revolt if I tried to stop, I'd feel that I was having heart attacks, I'd have diarrhoea, pains all over, my head would feel as if it was going to explode, I'd be beating a track to him every day. His best advice was to cut down to half, and stay—live—on that amount.

I couldn't accept that. Drugs were dominating me. I was popping them while I was with him in the surgery. Bizarrely, I was taking more than ever in order to allow me decide I wanted to stop. So I started cutting down. I started emptying the powder from inside the capsules and taking a bit out, but I couldn't quantify it. Sometimes I'd be knocking half out and sometimes three-quarters, and I was getting frustrated by not knowing how much I was or wasn't taking. I decided to ring around hospitals to find the same meds in smaller doses. Eventually, a pharmacist from a children's hospital mentioned how they measure small doses for very young children with a precise measuring spoon, so I got my hands on one of those.

I started working down my amounts myself, but I was hitting very low and desperate situations. One day I was listening to the radio and there was a lady talking about addiction, so I rang her. She said institutions wouldn't take me in for any sort of treatment, because I wasn't actually off the stuff. She suggested I go to NA.

'Aw Jesus, that's not for me,' I said.

'Listen, you rang me looking for my professional advice and I'm giving it to you. Ring this phone number and find out where is the nearest meeting to you tonight. Go to that meeting and then keep going for ten meetings before you decide whether you are in the right place or not.'

That was important, you see, because she didn't give me any rigmarole and she wasn't taking any crap from me. I rang the number.

I was at a very low point because I wasn't feeling well, and cutting down the drugs was actually hitting me very badly. So I went to my first NA meeting. I cried in the car going to that meeting, cried about where my life was going, my home, my home town, the people I knew and how I was held in such high esteem. I went into the meeting and it confirmed what I thought of drug addicts. They were scumbags. They were people that I didn't regard as being like me, in any way—badly bred, uneducated social misfits, talking about stealing handbags.

The only thing that I can remember about that night was that I didn't want to be there. I wanted nothing whatsoever to do with these people. It was all about injecting this and that, and 'I had to put it in my groin' and all this sort of stuff. I didn't mug somebody or have to beg for money, so I felt superior. But of course I'm forgetting the fact that I stole drink from where I was working and the money out of the till and all of that. And the fact that, at this stage, I would have been prepared to do everything that they did and more to fill my prescriptions, if I had to.

While I was there fighting the urge to run out of the room, I read the First Step and it said something like: 'We admit that we are powerless over addiction and our lives have become unmanageable.' I sat there and the word 'unmanageable' kept coming back to me all the time. Against all the odds, a couple of days later I decided I was going to go again because I couldn't get the word 'unmanageable' out of my mind.

No matter how smart I was, or how good my background was, or my social thing, or my profession or anything like that, I was actually in a similar situation to those scumbags. I didn't like them. These were exactly the kind of people that I wouldn't ever be seen with. But I couldn't manage my life and they couldn't manage their lives. We had something huge in common.

I dragged myself to another meeting and then I saw this God business in it. I had long given up on God and on going to Mass. So seeing this God factor coming into it made me feel it was not a runner for me. But still I kept going to meetings because my life was unmanageable. So I was going to the meetings but I was ready to crack up. The rest of my time was spent sitting at home measuring out my meds with my trusty little spoon and going nowhere else.

I started going to meetings that were in the leafy suburban areas of Bray and Stillorgan. Some of the people there were successful in business, but what came across to me was that these people had done an awful lot of very bad things and the word 'scum' came very much to mind here too.

I found that in the up-market suburbs people were talking about the demise of their business partnerships and high-class problems, but at this stage I was suffering very badly on a very basic level. I was in pain. So, unbelievably, I started doing a lot of inner-city meetings because the people there seemed to be suffering more and they were calling it as it was. I found I could identify with what they were saying much more, and I actually fitted in better. My mother would have been horrified!

I got a sponsor at NA who was fantastic, but I couldn't manage to get myself to his house the first few times. I was just so desperate and messed up. He used to meet me on a beach and we would just talk. From this point it took me the guts of eleven months to stop using. I was going to NA and little by little by little coming off the drugs, reducing my daily dose, applying my mind and logic to weaning myself off. After nearly a year, I was down to the tiniest amount per day—negligible really. It couldn't have been having any effect on me, but I couldn't let go. The letting go and jumping off was a massive step.

I decided not to take that step immediately as it was Christmas and I always found that a very difficult time as it brings up all this family business. A guy at NA was having a gathering and he encouraged me to come along. It took absolutely everything that I was made of to get to his house—to leave my house. I remember sitting there, in his living room, holding on to the leg of the table to steady myself, saying nothing, just looking at people coming in and going out. Here were people that I recognised, famous people that were involved in the media and very well-known in the city, involved in everything, and I'm sitting there saying to myself, 'Jesus, this is great because I'm not at home staring at the television by myself with the curtains pulled.' It was absolutely wonderful. Later that day I went to an NA meeting and then we all came back and played charades. A better Christmas I never had.

The twenty-first of January 2000 was my first clean day. The pains in every joint in my body, the waking up in a pool of sweat at night, the lack of control over the anger and fury building up inside—those weeks were a nightmare. One night, I started beating the wall in the corner bedroom in my house, the furthest wall away from the neighbouring house. I started breaking the wall, skinning my knuckles. The anger suppressed for so long was unleashing itself.

I bought a step machine and I would do at least 3,000 steps in a go. I would get up on it at night and I would call my mother every cunt under the sun. I know 'cunt' is not a nice word, but that's how it was. Her and all the neighbours, especially the women that I grew up listening to. I wouldn't sleep at night and I was having panic attacks; major panic attacks. My head was swimming with all the memories of my parents, my fears, the criticisms, my people-pleasing, my childhood, the lack of sparkle in my life, the lack of closeness or any love, the absence of friendship with my brothers, all of that. People outside might have thought a family with four boys would have been great craic to grow up in, but that wasn't the case at all. Each of us had our own things to deal with. I watched the movie *Sleepers* the other night about a couple of young friends and the camaraderie they shared. Jesus, I cried so much about my own life.

The first time that I ever had a massive outpouring on that one was when John Hume got the Nobel Peace Prize. I watched a programme about him and I saw that Hume had had the balls to actually get out and do exactly what he wanted to do. He had the balls to stand up and be counted and to plough his own furrow. I look back on my life and I see that the things I have achieved were not for the right reasons.

I'm still with the same company—I'm a partner now. The other senior partners know I've taken a hit, but they don't know what. When I started back at work, I came in through the fire escape because I couldn't face the reception area. I would bring a polystyrene cup with me and urinate into the cup, and then pour it out through the window so that I wouldn't have to meet anybody in the loo. I went in for an hour a day at the start. I suppose people would have felt that I was working outside the office but I've never discussed it with anybody.

Even talking about it here and now in these opulent surroundings, the darkness and the bleakness and the loneliness and the pain are as palpable as they ever were. I would have to say now that 90 per cent of the time I feel that I'm very fortunate, really blessed. Having a romantic relationship is the ultimate test. It's the last 'hurdle' for a recovering addict to cross. There is nothing that will actually get to the fundamental root of your recovery and test it more than an intimate relationship.

There is something outside of me that is actually supporting me. I don't know if that's what people call their God. All I can say is this: I can't tell you what it is because it's not 'God' as I understood Him or as I had been taught to fear Him growing up.

One winter's night when I was struggling with coming off my medication and I was in desperately bad form, I went for a walk along the cliff in Howth. Out of the blue, without thinking of anything, I got this hugely warm feeling. No voices, no lights, nothing like that, but this very real feeling of my father being beside me. My father, the loving gentle guy who adored us boys quietly and was always dignified. If there is an afterlife and there is good in it, then he is part of it. From that night on the beach, I started to talk to him and I get great comfort from it. I would never talk to my mother at all. I don't suppose she ever set out to do anything wrong or bad, she was a product of where she came from, but I would find no comfort in turning to her.

My relationships with my brothers are completely dysfunctional. We aren't equipped to reach each other. I was away last Christmas and I met my brothers for New Year's Eve. I had this rage inside me when I heard the crap we were all going on with. It came to twelve o'clock and the most we could actually do was shake hands. Within five minutes of midnight, they all left. We're emotional cripples. None of us knows what to say to each other, how to be, how to feel.

I have to accept that we are what we are. We are all playing with the cards we have been dealt.

I still go to meetings every Friday evening and at least one other during the week. For about two years after I was clean, I used to go around shaking hands with everyone at meetings, maybe eighty people. The business façade was still with me. One night I was sitting over in the corner and I didn't want to shake hands with anyone. I was kind of wondering if I was in bad form, but it wasn't that. It was actually that I had started to finally, for the first time in my life, lose the need to be the crowd-pleaser.

————

'Addiction is so insidious that it determines where the drug user goes on holidays, who they spend time with, what they do for the week ahead, what they do every day, where they have their lunch.'

Gerry Hickey is a psychotherapist and counsellor. The effect of addictions and addiction itself take up two thirds of his practice on Dublin's Adelaide Road. His clients are largely professional men and women with prescription-drug and street-drug addictions. They're private clients and most are referred by their GP.

Living in an environment where the one-size-fits-all principle is applied inevitably leaves some people feeling they don't fit in. And isolation comes automatically through feeling different. Most people who get a hit from their first use of drugs and alcohol will tell you that for the first time they thought: 'Wow! I fit in.' The world changed; they didn't have to change anymore; the world changed for them. They feel confident, they've got everything; the hit gives them this incredible comfort and pleasure. Everything they'd tried to do and feel all their lives, they've suddenly got in this few minutes. That's the big attraction.

Chemical addiction, psychological addiction and emotional addiction often follow. In time, the drug takes over like a big gorilla and chains the person onto it, so where the drug decides to go the person follows. My job is to try to turn that gorilla into a smaller little chipmunk on their shoulder and to keep it there; it doesn't ever go away, but I try to prevent it ever developing into a gorilla again.

Two things become entangled for successful, professional individuals who abuse drugs: one is the grandiosity of living life itself and doing well and being seen to be accomplished, and the other is the darkness, what goes on when the shades are pulled down or when they wake up in the morning after a binge and feel the uncertainty and the insecurity. There's a multitude of horrible things and negative fears that go with addictive behaviour.

Even though drug abusers can appear to be living normally, the insidiousness of their addiction is always being fuelled and facilitated by their lies and secrets, by their shame and embarrassment. They don't want to blow the cover on their use; they want to appear to be normal. So they lie. They lie to everybody, in particular to those close to them. The initial reaction of loved ones is denial, so they buy into the lies. At work, within friendships and relationships, lies become the norm, the way to maintain the façade.

Just as there is shame and stigma attached to drug abuse, there is shame and stigma attached to recovery. People attend my practice here in Dublin from Waterford, Galway, Belfast and all over the country rather than be seen going through the door of their own local counsellor. I'll regularly pick out a new client coming up the road with the lapels of their coat up and a hat pulled down, or wearing old-style Hollywood sunglasses and a headscarf. They don't de-frock until they're safely inside.

To recover, an addict needs identification with individuals of similar thinking. I do think that 'class' is important to recovery. We're too politically correct sometimes in that area. Life history, background, lifestyle—all of those ingredients form a very important part of identification. That said, it's true that addicts from all walks of life end up in the same gutter.

————

'I had always been confused about my sexuality and very, very uncomfortable even with sexual energy. For much of my life, I laboured under this sheer and unspeakable horror that I might be gay, because I came from a place where gays were considered shameful freaks and the worst kind of sinners. You certainly didn't want one in the family.'

Formerly the Head Designer of a prestigious design agency in London, Grace Cleary is now a practising psychotherapist. She lives alone in a beautiful old house on the Dingle Peninsula. She is forty-four years old and 'clean and serene' since the late 1990s.

On my last big night out, I thought I was going to be murdered. It was a real shock the next day when I remembered bits back and saw where drugs had taken me. I was in a right state coming out of a bar when I went in to this little taxi company that I knew to be a bit dodgy. I got into a taxi and came on to the taxi driver. I ended up somewhere in a terrifying backstreet in a part of London that I didn't know with this brutish, horrible man on top of me shouting obscenities. The whole thing was horrific. My self-disgust could not have been greater; it was as if all of the pain and depression and the meaninglessness of life peaked somehow that night and I knew I couldn't live that way anymore.

A funny thing was that despite only being interested in women, when I was out of my skull on drink and drugs I had sex with men. One-off seedy sex. And that is often the nastiest side of addiction for women. It can be the worst thing to live with. And it's often the reason why you just keep on using, because you can't bear to be with yourself when you think of the monstrosities that you were with, and the things you did, hours and days before. So much of drug use is about self-hatred and self-denigration. My sober relationships were with women and my drug-fuelled hazes were with brutal men. I'm not suggesting I was a victim. In fact, I would have been looking for it, looking for men, when I was out of it.

I'm from a small town in County Fermanagh—quite a middle-class, mixed Protestant and Catholic area where everybody knows everybody else. I have three brothers, so I was the only girl—and the youngest child. We were a fairly conventional set-up. My father had a good job and was esteemed by the neighbours and my mother was the quintessential proud housewife. Both Catholics, my parents had come from very country backgrounds and moved into the town and they had huge aspirations for us, their children, to be educated. It was the North of Ireland in the 1960s and 1970s; education was the way out of the unsettled situation. My parents put huge emphasis on our success. I suppose I had one of those Irish Catholic childhoods that appears honest and healthy, but underneath there is a lot of damage. There were a lot of really good things. I try to be more balanced about it in my mind now. It was a very beautiful area to grow up in, I had access to a lot of green space and beauty, I had friends on my doorstep, and my parents were good people.

But under the veneer, there was other stuff. There was silence and there was sexual abuse. I was abused by a neighbour from when I was about six years of age until I was eleven, which I think had a huge impact on me growing up. I'm not blaming my addictions on it, but I do think it certainly affected my sense of my place in the world. I had a dark and sad secret that I couldn't tell.

I started drinking at seventeen. It was the early 1980s and there was nothing going on, only pubs. I loved it actually, the old pubs near my home with the fires and the cosy atmosphere; I was really drawn to it. As soon as I had a drink, I felt different. By different, I mean better. Much better. I didn't mind the incredible downhill spiral afterwards, the sickness later that night, the write-off that the next day would be. It was worth it for the incredible peak I felt beforehand. All of my friends at home drank lots, all of us. I was no different within this group.

Later in my life, I realised this. I had my friends from London, and from work, and from university, and friends I made through other avenues, and I kept them apart from my childhood friends from home. I deliberately rarely mixed them, unless I couldn't help it. I think I knew that the drinking with the home group was rather excessive. I definitely drank more and took drugs more with the Irish lot.

I legged it to university in Wales when I was eighteen to study psychology, and in one way I was absolutely delighted to get out of the North, but in another I was completely bereft. I felt like a fish out of water. I was always plagued by the sense that someone was going to catch me out—that I shouldn't be there. I was incapable of being comfortable. I carried around a sense of unease. In some ways, I suppose, alcohol was already a problem at this stage, in so far as I was drinking to get drunk most nights, and I was always the most drunk of the group. I felt like I could really relate to people when I was drinking and I found it easy to be in company then. I was studying psychology, of course! Studying why people do the things they do.

On the whole, I was happy there, away from the clutches of my parents, who were very traditional, and the small town mentality. Both of my parents were pioneers so they thought that any drinking was excessive. It was a great freedom.

I was in Wales for five years. On one level, I was plodding along, just a student experimenting with drugs, experimenting with sexual partners. On another level, it was a time—one of very many—of incredible anxiety and feeling like I didn't fit anywhere. Constant low-grade anxiety and fear of everything.

Academically, I did okay, although my socialising adversely affected my grades and my attendance. I would get shockingly drunk and take pills, dope, whatever was around. I'd do outrageous things that were always great for the telling by the others the next day. Numerous scrapes I got myself into. Sure, they were all great tales for later on.

I found one of my diaries recently and, really, it was every single night. The diary wasn't a record of my emotional life or things that were happening to me. It was purely a social schedule—a necessary one, I had so much going on. Life was about going out and getting absolutely wrecked and having wild craic. The progression with drugs started to take me to other places soon after. I would get ferociously angry when I was using drugs. All of the secretive stuff from my past would well up inside me and I'd be like a demon. And I'd be sick, unable to move, and pass out and I'd have black-outs—absolutely no recollection of anything that I'd have said. I started doing this bargaining with myself that I'd only have X amount the next day, but then the day would wear on and I couldn't do it. I had no control—I'd have to drink and take whatever drugs were going.

I had a long-term relationship with another student, Ray, which survived until after we graduated. We went to London and he was working for a very successful firm that only took on the cream of graduates. So he got this very high-powered position, within this global corporation which regularly did exclusive weekends and tea dances in country clubs for their staff. It was desperately false and contrived, all of it. I couldn't stand it. He was fine with it and very concerned about his performance and his image and his background and the corporate ladder. They would take part in these incredibly competitive games that seemed to me to be just about humiliating each other, so even the 'entertainment' was uncomfortable and revolting.

The first outing I went to with him in the Waldorf Hotel, I was in a bad way from the night before and I remember my hands shaking so much that I couldn't lift the champagne glass off the waiter's tray. But once I had drunk that first glass, I could have walked around the whole night with my glass perched between my two fingers. Ray went mental with me later that evening because he felt that in my dinner table conversation with his new boss I didn't come off as ambitious enough, that I didn't have enough of a plan for my life. They all wanted to rule the world before they were thirty and I didn't. I got completely pissed that night because I couldn't handle the situation at all. My drinking did play a large part in the break-up of our relationship but I didn't see it as a problem; I was young, from a nice family, and graduating with Honours. I wasn't in the gutter. He ended up getting an opportunity in Dubai, which was absolutely his thing—sunshine, the pool, people dancing attendance on him—he really wanted all of that. So that was the end of us.

I graduated and got a trainee management job with a very large multinational, where I was the only woman working with a crowd of Indian and Asian men. It was horrific. I only took it because I didn't know how to say no. I was living by myself in Surrey and I felt I was having the soul sucked out of me, working long hours and having a day off during the week when nobody else was off, so using drugs alone at home really took off then. Although I went on to far worse things, it was probably the darkest period of my life because I had had so much hope and had just graduated and everyone was talking about careers and I knew I was going nowhere on every level. Theoretically, I had my whole life in front of me and I was entirely miserable. But I didn't want to be back in the North.

My great friend Alex was from a very wealthy family. He grew up with an incredible entitlement—he had no doubt whatsoever that he could get from life what he wanted. And the contrast with me and my background of Northern Irish unworthiness was quite striking. I was having this job/career crisis, and he asked me what I liked, and advised me simply to do that. I couldn't believe that was an option. You think about what interests you and then you decide to do it? All my life, I'd always wanted to write a book or be in publishing, so I rewrote my CV and got a job in a publishing house in London City. I moved in with a friend in Hammersmith, and I felt my life might actually take off then.

The publishing house was full of young, dynamic people and every single one of them was Irish, even the MD, so I felt much more at home. The downside of this was that there was a huge drinking culture. It was incredible. At lunchtime we'd all head down to the pub and it'd be liquid lunches all round. And I'd end up on the missing list that night having followed all of the drink with a handful of pills and ended up lost in some other part of London, completely sick. I'd be too sick to go to work the next day, too sick to even think about ringing in. On a few occasions I didn't make contact for three days in a row. Once, I arrived in at about 1 p.m. on the fourth day and went straight to the pub to meet everyone on their lunch. When I was questioned about where I'd been, I just brushed it off laughing with, 'Oh, it's a long story!' and carried on. For ten years I smoked dope all day long, every day. I never went to work without being absolutely stoned. And if I was paranoid and nervous to begin with, this didn't help.

My immediate boss, Norah, was a total alcoholic and a drug abuser. I realise this now. She told me at the time that she hired me because I was Irish and there was always a great social side to the Irish. She and I got on brilliantly and holidayed together. She did pull me up on my timekeeping a couple of times, but never too seriously. My drinking and drug use was starting to really impact on my life now. I simply could not get anywhere when I was supposed to be there. I was missing important events, both personal and for business. All the promises to myself and to others—nothing held up in the face of LSD, ecstasy, any nasty pills, anything that would take me out of reality.

Working in publishing, I would always get given tickets for the theatre and I was regularly at book launches and media gatherings. So an evening might start off well enough with the theatre and dinner, perhaps. But despite any amount of promises I made to myself, I would invariably end up in a dangerous and seedy drug-fuelled situation alone. I could wake up in an alleyway, in the back of a taxi by myself, or on a tube shuttling along in the dark to God Knows Where. Some of my friends would say they were quite envious of my lifestyle because what they saw from the outside seemed like non-stop fun and adventure, but it wasn't like that at all.

I wasn't achieving my potential by any stretch of the imagination. My Northern friends and I had grown up with parents who just wanted us to have brass plates with our names on them; to be educated and to achieve. My mother had started to wonder why I wasn't making more of a name for myself at this stage with my degree and my intelligence, and I would try to dress up my career path when I would speak to her, but you couldn't pull the wool over my mother's eyes. I'm sure that my parents knew what was going on but they said nothing. I remember once I was stupid enough to bring drugs home on the plane. And my mother found them—a big bag of LSD—where I had dropped it down the back of the couch. It was part of my risk-taking and not caring. They were both pioneers and led very straight lives. I thought their lives were so grey and drab and dreadful. I couldn't bear that kind of existence. My whole being wanted some energy and expression and fun. Not the restrained and rigid 'good' lives that they lived.

But I wasn't happy at all, because under the surface there was an emotional turmoil—a total, almost palpable, unease and anxiety.

I'm sure I was also depressed from the sheer amount of chemicals and depressants I was shovelling into my body on a daily basis. When I was actually present in my office, I was good at my job and I had a natural flair for writing and design. I started to move more toward the artistic side of things. I was managing to get my work done. This is something that people outside often don't realise. Most alcoholics and drug users are 'functioning' users, in so far as they do turn up and they get the job done. They are the person next to you at work. Sometimes they might turn in late and look a bit peaky, but they may well be the person who seems to be succeeding within the company.

I had started to feel uneasy about the amount of drugs I was taking, only because I was realising that I couldn't stop—not even for one day. But I didn't talk to anyone about this, any of my friends. There was too much at stake—to be seen to be doing well, having all the trappings, to be dining in the right places, and to be having a good time. I was very affected by the people in my life and I had all of these very different groups of people that I was a part of, so I became chameleon-like, blending into whatever was expected of that group. Of course I was also drinking and popping pills before I showed up to meet any of them, so I was a high chameleon. It was a very watery kind of existence. I had no sense of what I was or what I liked. I was this fluid and floating mass.

It was also costing me absolutely every penny that I earned. I was constantly in overdraft, despite a very good income. No amount of money would have been enough. I could have spent two, three, ten times what I earned, with no difficulty at all. It was utterly chaotic. I was working and I was middle class so I had the facility of bank overdrafts and credit cards, and I exploited every angle with gay abandon.

The whole scene at work had got a bit too close and squalid. I used to go out partying with the MD a lot and relations between us had got a bit too confused and became very uncomfortable. He had a way of drawing me out, of asking me questions about my past, when I was high as a kite and ready to talk to anyone who would listen, in a horrendous, cloying, self-pitying kind of way. At this stage of my life in particular—I was reliant on drugs for about eleven years now—all of the ugliness of my past was right at the forefront of my mind and would come spilling out with ease. And I'd get angry and there would be chaos. And then we'd have to work together the next day, so perhaps he wanted me out then too. I left and landed this fantastic job managing a design agency in London. Of course I got sterling references—one glowing lie after another—from all my drinking buddies in publishing.

The design agency was a fantastically civilised place to work—I was the only Irish person! It was a beautifully designed, thriving company in Camden, by the canal. A French chef would come in and cook lunch for us every day. I had a very senior position so I really was the Great Pretender now, well capable of the job if I was in my full senses, but it wouldn't take long for me to drop the ball if I wasn't.

Life was now dominated by the business of alcohol and drugs. When I wasn't actually taking them, I was planning when and where I'd get them. Every day from lunchtime on, I was scheduling my evening—making calls to anyone and everyone to make sure I had someone to meet, somewhere to go. It wasn't because I felt like socialising or because I particularly wanted to catch up with this person. It was just so I could drink and take drugs without sitting alone. I could fool myself into thinking that I was having a normal night out, like the stooge who was with me. It never occurred to me to go home or to stay in for one evening. Sometimes, when I'm at home now on a Saturday watching *Tubridy Tonight*, I think of that and laugh at myself.

I was managing to survive the job and I got on well with everyone. I was often late, but I was the boss so I invented meetings and the like. I was falling asleep on the train home after nights out and ending up in places like Guildford or some tiny town in the middle of Surrey at all hours. I'd be stranded until morning. I'd then have to get home and ready, and only then start my commute to work. It was madness, but even though I'd be dying inside, when I'd tell one of my friends the next day, I'd make it sound like great craic, you know. It would all be for the telling. When I hear people do that now, I feel a kind of sadness for them because I know what's going on behind the story.

I started having a relationship around this time with a female colleague whom I found myself head-over-heels in love with. Although it felt entirely natural to be with her, it also felt absolutely wrong. I had unfathomable difficulty with it. From my background, I was massively uncomfortable with it. I would look on in horror and admiration as gay women were openly 'gay' with each other. At this stage, I knew I was gay and, since Ray, any flings I had had were with women. But I was never able to cope with it, although it was what I wanted.

I was desperately immature inside and the idea of opening up my heart to someone and having a functioning relationship—I simply wasn't capable of it. When we did eventually split up, I couldn't have given a shit … I was just so emotionally detached from it all; and from myself.

I stayed 'in the closet' for many years, but often, in my mind, I planned a very considered and dignified exit. There'd be tears and laughter and hugs and I'd give a splendid 'I am what I am' speech. Naturally, however, I came tumbling out of said closet obnoxiously drunk and high as a kite in the arms of some woman in front of many old friends from home. In one way I was relieved because it had felt like I had been holding in this dirty, shameful secret that had permeated my entire being for so long, but then in another, it was out there now; another black mark on show for all to see.

After some time I came under massive pressure in this working environment where people actually worked and looked to me to guide them. I was running out of excuses so I decided to set up on my own and I got a lot of work from clients of the company. Now I was on my time and my clock, which suited me a lot better. This set-up provided me with wonderful scope to indulge my drug habit. Not having any structure to the day is a bad, bad freedom to be afforded to a drug user. My rates were much higher, so I tripled my salary overnight. I got huge clients with great portfolios and big budgets but I was spending much of my time staring past my Mac and into space wondering, searching, thinking about drugs, worrying about life, plagued by this constant, latent feeling of being lost and sad and anxious, turning my past over in my head. I was stoned.

Some days, I'd suddenly become aware of this unbearable loud beeping noise and would wake, startled, to find that I had passed out on my computer, flat onto the keyboard and sent the cursor flying about and making this incredible piercing sound. This was me freelancing and earning my own money.

I felt like an absolute shit thinking about all the things I had done over the previous years, the people I had hurt, my parents and their aspirations. I became consumed by enormous guilt. I desperately wanted to set things to right with them and to be restored in their eyes, because I knew I was badly tarnished. So I decided to open up to them and shatter the silence by explaining to them what had happened to me for five years as a child. That would surely clean the slate and I would be the shining daughter again. This, my mess of a life, was all *his* fault. It became my reason to explain all of it—drink, drugs, sexual misadventures, everything. I had no sense of taking responsibility for any of my actions. I would unburden myself of this shame and the revelation would exonerate me.

So I went home to tell my parents. And it was devastating. Devastating for me, and for them, particularly for my dad. The man who abused me was a neighbour, a friend of the family. So it was a very tricky situation, and he was still in the house from time to time. They didn't know how to handle it. They said nothing. They did nothing. I'm sure they felt plenty, but they didn't articulate it.

But then, suddenly, one day a few weeks later, there was a little opening. My mother rang me up, just for a chat. It was only a tiny light, but I could see it. For years and years and years my relationship with her had been utterly closed—no communication, no feeling—battered by so much hurt and scorn from me. Our common bond was one of mutual loathing. She had never before rung me for a chat, and I'd never before heard her speak to me with a smile in her voice. I was overjoyed.

But then she died. Suddenly and shockingly two days later. It was five weeks since I had told her my terrible secret. At the time, I had urged her to confide in a friend, which she must have done. Somehow, the word got out, and there was a lot of talk at her wake and at her funeral about what I had told her, and how the shock of it had killed her. Her friends were part of a very small and proper community in Northern Ireland—so protective of secrecy and denial and so adept at hiding things—and yet this became a great topic of conversation. I suppose they felt that, now she was dead, they didn't need to be discreet. I spent the day of the funeral numb, except for a ferocious hangover that I was fighting.

The story became common knowledge and grew legs and our family was literally the talk of the town. It further devastated my poor father who was grieving for his wife and worrying about me. My brothers also found it very difficult. The parish priest became involved. The man in question was still living one street over and his neighbours went to the police. And, can you believe it, he had a heart attack within a week or so. As a story, it just got better. Everyone was getting off on the macabre drama of it all. The town had never been so awake.

My mum's sisters and brothers blamed me for her death. If I had just kept quiet, none of this would have happened. Did I realise that what I had told her had killed her? Why hadn't I just kept my big mouth shut? Why did I have to be so selfish? And did I know that I was also to blame for (my abuser) Geoff's heart attack and his failing health?

When I came back from London for my mother's month's mind Mass in September, the police were waiting to interview me about my claims. I was on the absolute edge. Between the shock of my mother's death and having to speak openly for the first time about the years of sexual abuse—it was horrendous.

The fact that I had thought telling my parents this secret would make everything okay was laughable now. It had only been a matter of weeks and so far the fall-out was that my mother was dead, I was in a police station being interrogated, there was a child abuser fighting for his life in hospital, and none of us could go outside the door without some neighbour or other voicing their little opinion. It was the complete opposite of okay. It hit me then, definitely and entirely, that in this world, silence and secrecy are the way to go.

I went home to London, but I wasn't sleeping at all. I was all over the place and so began my cocaine use. Despite all the drugs I had thrown into my body, I had always been wary of coke. That first week back home, I took it four days in a row. On top of the usual load of alcohol, cannabis and ecstasy. The following week, I was walking down the street one lunchtime when I started to hallucinate. The amount of chemicals in my body, combined with the stress of the police and the idea of a trial, and lack of sleep—I think my mind was really going. Within three weeks of utter hell and constant drug use, I ended up in therapy, of my own accord and out of sheer desperation. I couldn't live with feeling that I had caused my mother's death. The massive guilt I had felt already, combined with this, was just too much.

I went to therapy, not because I felt I had a drug problem or anything, but rather to deal with the whole nightmare I felt I had caused.

As luck would have it, my therapist, unbeknownst to me, was a recovering addict herself and had the measure of me the minute she saw me come through the door. The second time I went to see her I was still up from the previous day. I had left the house after lunch to go drinking, I had taken a handful of ecstasy pills in the afternoon, then a tonne of speed as the evening wore on, followed by about a gram of coke and then more pills and so on. It was now taking all of my time, what mental energy I had left, and all of my money to endeavour to manage a cocktail of substances to chase that temporary high, where life felt manageable for a few minutes. And then I turned up for my therapy session. I told her I was a bit hungover.

From that session on, she started to ask me about my alcohol and drug intake and to look at the role of these substances in my life. I didn't know what she was talking about. A short time later, she told me she couldn't work with me until I got myself clean. The therapy was going nowhere because I'd leave each session, go and get high and not deal with anything. Because that's how I lived. Drink and drugs to avoid reality. I had self-medicated since I was seventeen years old. And the one time in my life when I had tried being honest and speaking up, look what had happened.

She recommended a treatment programme for me in London and after some time I actually rooted out the number she had given me and signed myself up. I was so broken and on the edge that I felt I was losing my life, such as it was. I did feel a bit ridiculous because I was 'Irish'. I felt I could claim extra special knowledge of 'having a good time' because it's what we're known for. To admit yourself into treatment for too much of a good time seemed like a bit of a failure really. It took me a long time to get over my superiority with regard to drink and drugs and to finally realise that I needed help. When I did eventually articulate it, it came out in these terrifying, almost primal sobs.

Geoff died soon after. I was relieved that he was gone and that we could all pretend to go back to a better time of denial when we didn't have to deal with what his existence reminded us of. I spent two years in an addiction programme—the first stage of which was a closed, residential programme—with total abstinence from everything from day one. Within that early stage Christmas came around and I went home to Fermanagh for two days because it was the first year my mother wouldn't have been in the house. It was desperate. The last 'substance' I ever had was a glass of wine over that Christmas period. I didn't want it anymore. The desire to use had left me. I couldn't bear it to be the fuel for my life any longer. It was just a destructive force. I had turned a corner in my head and I knew I needed to be strong now for myself and for my father. After seventeen years in the grip of one substance or another, I was actually 'released' from addiction quite quickly in the end and I'm so grateful for that.

My dad died while I was in my programme, but at least he had seen me clean and sober. He was happy about that. They never knew I was gay, either of my parents. Or if they did, they certainly never broached the topic. I could never ever have had that kind of discussion with them. My sexuality was so encased in shame that any mention of sex or sexuality just brings about these absolute and unadulterated feelings of disgrace and embarrassment; I'm very aware of them even talking about it here today.

During my time in treatment, a lot of people came and went, and by the time I reached the end of my programme, only two of us out of nineteen had made it. All of the others left early, went back out and picked up where they had left off. One of my friends died. She was found on the floor of her apartment a couple of days after she checked herself out.

When I finished treatment in 1997 I did a five-year degree in psychotherapy. I have a lot of faith in the value of therapy, but I do believe that to recover from the kind of lifestyle that I had there has to be something more to get you through. Some kind of spiritual dimension—whatever that may be for you—is necessary;

something bigger and outside yourself and beyond addiction that you can believe in.

Having come through Catholicism, however, I certainly wasn't on the market for another religion. I started to meditate and to read about spirituality. I spent time at the Dzogchen Beara Spiritual Care Centre in West Cork while I was in recovery, and I found it just wonderful. I loved their approach and my time there was a really positive turning point.

I came back to live in Ireland, here in Dingle—I couldn't ever bear to go back home—in 2002 and got a position as a psychotherapist. I see people who are perceived to be successful, life's 'winners', grappling with drug addiction all of the time.

———

*'When I first went for treatment for my addiction,
I was fully expecting my bag to be stolen.'*

Amy previously worked as an air traffic controller. She is thirty-nine years old and hasn't used drugs in over three years. Despite her upbringing in a very middle-class home, she lived in squalor for many years to avoid wasting money on rent or a mortgage, when it could be better spent on drugs.

I suppose the biggest pointer that I had a problem was the second pregnancy. I got pregnant in order to put an end to the terrible path I was on, and then I realised I couldn't get off the path. I saw that it was easier for me to terminate a second pregnancy than to stop using drugs. I think pregnancy and abortion are very prominent issues for many female addicts.

I was a couple of years clean before I could even attempt to deal with the regret that I felt or to contemplate having my own child.

My sister became pregnant and the grief that I had buried suddenly started to come to the surface, to totally consume me. I would wake up in the middle of the night—for a long time—sobbing and crying. After months, I suppose I started on the road to forgiving myself. I still have huge regret and huge sadness about the abortions, and I still cry when I think about it.

I worked for nine years as an air traffic controller, then made a career change and have been working in health care for the last three years. The majority of my using would have been in my days working out at the airport when I was doing shift work. My primary drug of choice would have been hash but I would certainly have gone on regular benders taking E and cocaine, whatever was available.

The first time I drank, it was the most horrendous experience. I was just thirteen and in the Gaeltacht in Donegal, and I just thought it was the thing to do: to knock back neat vodka. I remember getting literally blind drunk, and being aware of my surroundings, but not being able to see anything. I was sexually assaulted at that age because I was drunk. I was with older boys—all the girls wanted to hang out with the older boys. I picked myself up the next day and never spoke about it until I was thirty. I thought that was fine. I don't know where I ever got the warped idea I acted on for years that getting out of it on drink or drugs was fun.

I'm the oldest of three girls. My mother is a public health nurse and my father is an architect. I was drinking regularly from when I was fifteen—going to the pub and getting served. This continued for over a decade and then it was no longer enough for me. I started working as an air traffic controller when I was twenty-six and I started looking for drugs. I wanted something more than alcohol. That year, I got pregnant, because I was drunk and stoned and I didn't use contraception. I had an abortion and I didn't tell a soul.

I remember being on Leeson Street the night I came home from the clinic in London, dressed in this really short black dress with high heels and feeling devastated. I was looking for heroin, but I didn't know anyone who had it. I was in such pain I wanted something a lot stronger than the alcohol.

I didn't find heroin, but I found ecstasy and cocaine. And within weeks I was totally caught up in the rave scene. I would get really high and have a great seventy-two-hour weekend of using, and then plummet into horrendous depression for the rest of the week at work. I was doing shift work, so Monday would still be my weekend. I might work ten days in a row, then binge on drugs for three or four days.

I always actively sought out drugs. In my late twenties I had a really passionate affair with a guy who was all into his drugs, and I lived with him for a while. We used drugs together all the time. He was a wealthy guy with a really prestigious position, and it suited him to have me on his arm. We had an awful break-up and I really lost the plot altogether then. That time coincided with the disintegration of the group of using friends I had. One of them died of a heroin overdose and we all went our separate ways after that. It was a dreadful time. Her death didn't register with me as a drug-related incident, which is bizarre now when I think about it.

I wasn't using heroin, but I would have—if it had come my way. I think in some ways I was protected by some of the guys in the group who were doing it. I only realised this recently. I was never offered it and I knew what they were at and I wanted it. I got really jealous of anyone who was having a stronger high than me. One time my boyfriend took two E's and I only had one and I got so angry with him. I could just see he was far more out of it that I was. So it was like that. It was crazy.

My work life was suffering terribly now. I was really unreliable, always late, taking a lot of sick days, coming into work with a really bad attitude, feeling angry and really distancing myself from people at work. I felt work was a real inconvenience actually. I was obsessive about my actual work itself once I got there—I was always acutely aware of safety and precision—but my manner was the pits. The airport was a great place to work. Managers confronted me about my lateness and my sick leave many times, but it had no effect whatsoever. I didn't even hear it.

Eventually a supervisor confronted me and asked me if I had a substance abuse problem. I was outraged at her. The bloody cheek! I certainly did not have a problem, thank you. She was the one with a problem.

And yet every day was like getting into a fast car that I just couldn't stop. I was earning very good money, but living in the grottiest bedsit, the most horrendous accommodation, because it was as cheap as it was dirty. I wasn't going to part with a bean that could be more wisely spent on coke or hash. I had isolated myself totally, with not a friend in the world. There were a couple of guys I could use with, but I would be ashamed to introduce them to anybody. They were scumbags really. We had nothing else in common except getting out of our heads together. One guy was a full-time dealer. I met him in a pub one night and I hung out with him from then on because I knew he would supply me. I started running errands for him, bringing drugs in from London in my shoes. Walking past sniffer dogs in the airport; calm as you like. I wanted it so much that I was prepared to just take the chance. I couldn't grasp the reality of what would happen if I got caught.

I was using hash every day—morning to night—and then cocaine and ecstasy every other night. I was very clever about spotting people who might be selling. I was always on the lookout for more, for better quality. I think when you're using, you have this built-in radar where you can home in on others who are at the same thing. I can still tell today.

Work was a disaster at this stage. Younger colleagues were being promoted over me and it was all very uncomfortable. I really wanted to leave but I couldn't get it together to look for another job. I was causing major resentment at work, and rightly so, because I was pissing people off by coming in late. My time-keeping meant that they couldn't get home in time.

One night, when I was smoking with a guy that I was having a fling with, I came up with the answer to all of my problems. I'd get pregnant, and have a baby. That would surely put an end to all the madness. A baby would motivate me to clean up my act. I didn't involve him in the decision.

So I woke up one day soon after, pregnant and horrified. I knew I wouldn't be able to have a baby, to raise a baby. I couldn't believe I'd done it again. I knew this would kill me. I couldn't recover from a second abortion and yet I couldn't not have an abortion. So I did it again. I went over to London, I had another abortion and, about two months later, I hit absolute rock bottom.

Again, I told nobody. Now, I couldn't get out of it anymore. I couldn't get away from the feeling, the pain, the shame. I was smoking hash and using coke at home on my own at night. As soon as I came in from work, I'd get stoned immediately; I would-n't even have my work clothes off. I was feeling suicidal. I didn't want to wake up anymore.

One day at work everything came to a head, and I just felt like pulling my clothes off, pulling my hair out, and waiting for the men in white coats to come and take me away. I didn't see myself as a drug addict. I just knew I was in deep shit.

I started seeing a counsellor and he had me write my 'self story', starting from as young as I could remember until nineteen, at first. It was so sad—full of dreadful stuff that had happened because I drank and used drugs. So I used even more hash and E and coke to avoid dealing with the therapy. My counsellor told me I was an addict and that I was going to end up killing myself. I drove up to an NA meeting in the Rutland Centre that very night, fully expect-ing to get my handbag robbed. I was really afraid going in. I had the stereotype image of addicts myself, I just couldn't see how I would fit in there. I was very, very pleasantly surprised. I met people that I really related to, men and women in their thirties and forties and fifties from nice backgrounds.

I got clean very soon after that. I had a desperately difficult time but I didn't relapse. I'm drug-free nearly four years now. What was funny was that when I got clean I still couldn't make it into work on time, and I still had a lot of sick leave. Not using doesn't automatically make you better. I was six months clean when I left my job in the airport.

In my new job, I've never been late and I'm never off sick. Some of my close colleagues know that I'm in recovery, but I would only tell them I'm in Alcoholics Anonymous. I wouldn't ever say Narcotics Anonymous. Most people—no matter how progressive or open-minded—can't deal with having a recovering drug addict for a colleague.

Where I work now, I see an awful lot of addiction. I see the low end, several generations of addiction. It can be hard sometimes but it serves as a very stark reminder. I got married last year, to a man I met in NA actually! I didn't plan on meeting somebody at all, let alone in recovery. We've just had our first child, Melanie. Life isn't all roses. My husband and I both have dark ghosts that we carry around, but we're pulling through together.

I still cry about the babies I didn't have and I don't think I'll ever fully come to terms with my stupidity and my loss.

Chapter 6

Drugs Don't Wreck Lives, Hangovers Do

'Do you ever see a good drugs story on the news?
Never.
The news is supposed to be objective, but every drug
story is negative. Well hold it. I've had some killer
times on drugs. Let's hear the whole story.'
BILL HICKS, *RELENTLESS*

———

**Tom is a judge. He and his wife Eileen have three children. Tom
and Eileen regularly host dinner parties in their Georgian home
in one of Dublin city centre's trophy enclaves. Tom makes a trip
to the flats in Sheriff Street during these evenings to buy cocaine
and ketamine to share with their guests. Tom explains:**

The coke board is handed around early in the night to get things
going. The ketamine comes later—after the meal and toward the

end of the evening—so that guests are 'down' enough to drive and to face the babysitter when they get home. I see nothing wrong with it. Nobody has ever caused any trouble or had anything other than a great time. You wake up in the morning a lot clearer than if you'd had your fill of pints. I've yet to come across a guest who hasn't taken part.

———

'Drug dealers are good mathematicians. I know the price of everything and have had street training from all my dealing and owing and ripping clients and dealers off. I still look at things, items, and think, that'd get you X grams of cocaine or whatever. My clients included people from every white-collar profession—you name it: bankers, solicitors, engineers, teachers, politicians, even the country's top actors. People with big jobs and huge responsibility.'

Liam is a forty-year-old accountant. For nine years, he was a daily drug user and dealer.

The most bizarre incident of my whole sorry tale happened just over a year ago. I rang my mother because I'd just been threatened by a fairly big dealer that I owed a bit of money to. I'm thirty-eight years of age and I ring my mother to tell her I'm a drug abuser and a dealer and that I'm on my way over to her house to collect some money so that I won't get killed.

If I could have turned up the money—€8,000—any other way, I would have. But I had no time and was looking at a severe beating, the very best. I'd exhausted every other source I could think of. If paying this guy, and getting money for more drugs, meant spilling the whole drug thing to Mum, then so be it. How she might feel on hearing this bombshell didn't even pass through my head.

I remember having a three-hour meeting with her in the kitchen. There was a 'big talk' during which she cried and shouted and got hysterical. She kept saying, 'It has to finish. You're going to kill yourself,' and sobbing. I made her all the promises under the sun. I'd have said anything. I was lying, of course. But I got the money out of her. I remember thinking, 'I'll take the cash to him and sort it all out. I'll have a clean slate then, so I'll be able to get a bit more from him,' but it didn't happen like that.

She couldn't get cash in time so she had to write a personal cheque. And she insisted on coming with me.

So my mother and I went to Blanchardstown in her navy-blue people carrier. The journey seemed like a lifetime. She was still crying and raging at me and I was shouting at her about her driving and how we should have avoided the M50. It was vaguely comical in a way: My mum driving me to meet a guy with a baseball bat to pay off a drug debt with one of her personal cheques. I had to see if he would take the cheque. Made out to cash and signed by my sixty-four-year-old mother. It was madness, complete madness. There was a bit of hanging around when we got there—my mother parked down the road with the engine running—and I waited to see if he'd take the cheque. He was getting someone to cash it for him before I could leave. He wouldn't give me anything else. He didn't want to know me after this fiasco.

I suppose I come from quite a well-to-do family. My father is also in financial services and my mother is a university lecturer. The first drug that I found was butane gas in the science lab in school. I'd have been about fourteen when I started having a bit of craic with that. This was something that was a bit of a laugh but it was closely followed by regular use of solvents and glues. I enjoyed the out-of-body experience where I was no longer me, but at the same time I knew to maintain the grades and the good kid reputation.

By the time I was seventeen, I was drinking quite excessively and using all manner of solvents and aerosols. I'd be up at the bar ordering drinks and be drinking away at the bar before I'd come back down to the table. Coming from the trusting family that I did, money was always left lying around. I was always the one who was being carried home. When I started going to nightclubs I realised there was other stuff going around. In a flash, my weekends were spanning four days and nights and I was up to my eyeballs on ecstasy and speed. I wasn't a great drinker so the class-A's would prolong my ability to drink and that's where I felt I'd found paradise. I just thought, 'This is for me.'

I always held a job down. I had an image to keep. I'd always show up in work. Also, I always held a job down because I knew a job was money, and money was more drugs. There was always money if I needed it, you know. And that was a constant trend, being shipped out of debt, get myself into debt, overspending. I would build up debt within a group of friends and then move on to another group.

I felt that acceptance would be greater if I had the drugs myself, so I started shipping in speed myself from the North. Initially a couple of ounces twice a month. But I knew that the bigger the bag I had, the more friends I'd get. So I quickly upped my orders. I thought this was a fantastic buzz, I thought I was Al Capone.

The guy I'd buy from was pretty dodgy—I suppose he was what I became. I didn't know whether he was carrying a gun or not but he certainly looked like he might. It was a bit scary, but I remember that I always got butterflies when I was going to meet him. It was a great rush for a good boy from Greystones, so much so that it would actually sometimes cause me to be physically sick. I can feel it, I can still feel it now talking about it.

By the time I was twenty I was buying from a few guys and dealing on a bigger scale. My phone was always ringing and I was afraid to answer it because I was worried about who might be looking for me. I was also doing my accountancy exams in the evenings and still living at home. My parents knew nothing about all of the shenanigans that were going on. I was dressing well and maintaining the façade. Everything on the outside was dandy. I decided that home was holding my budding business back, so I moved in with a friend I'd known since I was a child.

I saw this move as a prime opportunity, a fantastic business opportunity to branch out. He didn't know what I was up to. I was very guarded about my secret life. I was using speed and ecstasy myself most days and selling to a regular clientele. I decided that cocaine was where the money was and started moving into that area. Before long I was using coke every day. I was always a bit of a schemer and managed to have something for myself. I was using in the morning, at work, in the evenings, all the time. But I still looked the part and I never missed a day at the office. I felt that what prevented me from having a drug problem or being an addict was that addicts were those who injected heroin and were unemployed. I had a career, nice clothes and money. I was obviously successful at life. Appearances were everything.

Financially, things were spiralling in all areas because I was always robbing Peter to pay Paul. There was always something on and I'd spend money extravagantly on clothes and cars and champagne. Then I'd have to find money for drugs. Invariably, money for rent was never found. I jumped from apartment to apartment, never staying too long, continuously running up bills and shafting a lot of people along the way.

I was bouncing lies all over the place. I was always one to network so I was forever trying to get the best deal. And I wasn't into dealing with Mickey Mouse dealers. I was dealing with the big boys. I was dealing with guys who would have killed me. I put myself in very serious situations. I didn't know really what I was dabbling with. I had to start moving from dealer to dealer because

I was ripping off so many of them that they just weren't going to deal with me. I was always scheming, planning to buy an ounce, sell a half, keep a half and make a bit of money and clear my debts. That never happened. Any profit I made just funded more drugs or more lavish suits.

I was always scheming. Sitting down every day to do my book-keeping: I'll get that off him and he'll give me this and she'll give me that. I'll run up a bill there and I'll get my parents to pay for that. Constant juggling.

On the outside I was doing all the right things. I was living with a girl I was now engaged to. I was going to buy a house and we were getting married in the summer. She had no idea about the real me. She was marrying a hologram. I was working away and I looked good. I was about thirty at this stage and my drug use was probably about ten years old. I was progressing now and getting quite adept at ripping my clients off. A lot more cocaine was going to personal use and then I was mixing the rest before I sold it on.

One day my fiancée went to the bank to withdraw a deposit for the Shelbourne Hotel from our wedding fund of €50,000 and discovered there was €80 in the account. Our relationship ended soon afterwards. I had spent it all, and I had borrowed at least that amount again. I had loans up to my ears. I might have had anything upwards of €120,000 worth of debt at this stage.

I started going up the North and dealing up there and bringing coke over the Border. I was invincible at this stage. During this time, my best friend died of a drug-related heart attack. Do you think that put me off? Not at all. My drug use went hard core after that. I started taking more. That wasn't going to happen to me. I was the king. I had a lot of solicitors' letters for debts from various banking institutions. I passed them on—usually to the bin. The Northern business got a bit hairy, even for me, so I started to scale that down. I was in a staunchly Protestant area, and they didn't like my D-reg. car and my Southern accent and flash clothes.

I was using cocaine now to an extreme degree. Whereas at the beginning it made me very efficient and enabled me to take on the world, that stage had passed and now I was having blackouts and dizzy spells and serious headaches and nosebleeds. I knew it was taking its toll on my body. But I was still presenting myself at work, never missing a day. I was running my drug business from my office phone and doing little else.

I was living in a nice suburb outside Dublin, ripping off another landlord who's a friend of the family. He's a fairly powerful solicitor and here was me thinking, 'Ha ha, I'm ripping you off.' Little did I know. My stupidity and arrogance were at an all-time high.

By now I'd had a run-in with a dealer and there were very serious shenanigans and threats going on. The evening I rang my mother for help, there had been a messenger guy in my front garden with a baseball bat waiting for me when I got home to tell me that I had twenty-four hours to pay off the debt I owed his boss. I only owed him about €8,000 but I'd no way of paying it. So, as I said, the mammy sorted it out. After he took her cheque, he put me in touch with someone who was an even bigger fish to see if I'd fuck with him. Of course I did. I thought, 'I'll just shaft him the once, and then I'll never shaft him again.' And I very nearly got myself killed.

I was exhausted now. Between the continuous drug use and the to-ing and fro-ing and phone calls and him and her and mine and the whole thing—it was like having a very demanding, full-time job.

The new dealer turned from Mr Nice Guy into someone who turns up in the pub you're in and shows you a firearm under the table. So I was on the phone begging again. This time I phoned my now-partner. But she wasn't interested in my drama and said she'd washed her hands of me. My one remaining lifeline was her brother. I thought he might help me out, for her. And he did. He came down on a motorbike and into the pub and gave me some cash. I didn't get the whole lot but I'd bought myself a bit of time.

I was inhabiting dodgy places now. And I was putting on the accent. I didn't realise how dangerous this whole situation was. I knew you wouldn't be bringing these people home to meet your parents, and it didn't really surprise me when this guy produced the gun. He said this was what he had to do because he was getting it at the other end. It was another couple of days before I actually got the full amount to him.

I continued using and borrowing and owing and scraping by. One night I ended up having a fight with a guy in a club and I jumped into my Land Rover in a rage and drove home full of everything—coke, ecstasy, drink—and I remember being really distraught and really upset. I woke up in St James's Hospital in Intensive Care. I'd crashed the jeep—written it off actually—and maybe killed someone in the process. And I can't remember a thing. I think I recall hitting a tree. When I woke up in the ward my stepson was looking in through the window at me in tears, and I'd love to say I had a moment of realisation or an epiphany, but I didn't. Seeing him heartbroken looking in at me just irritated me. I wanted to tell him to get off my back, with his tears. Nothing could stop me. The nurses were threatening me: 'We have a blood sample,' and I was telling them to fuck off and who did they think they were?

As it turned out, a judge lived on the road where I crashed and he stopped me from being breathalysed. He saved my bacon. He didn't know me. Maybe he liked the look of me or maybe it was my jeep.

I'd broken my chest bone and I'd dislocated my shoulder. I remember there being pain. This was to be the very first of many days absent from my office. I thought I was dying. I had time in there to calm down and to think about things. I felt quite content—I was being given morphine. Before I was discharged I remember saying to myself that I'd have one more lash of cocaine. *Just the one.*

I think I had about an eighth of an ounce left in my bedroom, which should have kept me going for most of a day. But I got home and just used it continuously. I remember being on my knees and crying, looking in the mirror at my bruised face and crying and hating myself and shouting, 'What the fuck is going on here?' I couldn't physically get myself out of that room. I couldn't get myself dressed. I couldn't wash myself. I couldn't do anything. I can't remember the sequence of events after that but I did get more coke and I ended up overdosing. I don't know whether it was intentional or not. At the time I knew what I was using was very, very substantial. I ended up back in hospital on a cardiac machine.

I haven't used drugs since that day. It's been the most horrific few months of my life trying to stay off them. I get myself to Narcotics Anonymous meetings at least twice a week. At the start I went once if not twice a day, every day and, because I wear a suit, I'd be taking the suit and tie off and putting on a jumper and jeans and going to meetings at lunchtime. I thought it'd be full of 'lads', you know? But the meetings I go to are full of professional people—other accountants, doctors, nurses, teachers. There's comfort in that. I don't feel like the only fucking idiot because I'm not the only one there who had advantages.

I'm always doing the private investigator. I can spot someone either waiting for a delivery, or who's in to meet someone, or someone who's dealing from a mile away. Those sightings really unnerve me. Drugs took me to some really scary and dark places. I had run-ins with dangerous people, got involved in dangerous activities and had close shaves with the police, but thankfully I'm here today and I don't have any charges outstanding. I still have my career, and nobody's ever mentioned my lifestyle or my car crash or the rumours about my substance abuse.

You hear about people in recovery saying, 'Oh I heard the birds singing for the first time in fifteen years.' I don't hear the birds singing at all. Well, if I do, I don't notice. But I do appreciate things like my stepson smiling at me and I'd hate to break his heart again.

That said, I'd use drugs now, today, if I thought that I could do so successfully. Ninety per cent of the best times of my life were when I was using drugs and partying. I have to keep reminding myself how bad it all became. If I was sixty-five and clean and thought that I might not have long left, would I start using again? Yes. Without a doubt.

———

'When I was forty-seven years old and had been clean for twelve months, I started a new position working for a very well-to-do family and there was a lot of coke going around. The arrangement was that they paid me half my fee in coke and half in cash, so of course I started using again. Back on the merry-go-round like I'd never been off it.'

Jane Feeney is a horticulturist, musician and gourmet chef. With many strings to her bow, she has been employed variously by upper-class Irish families as a modern-day butler, hosting dinner parties, caring for and tutoring children, and landscaping and tending to gardens. Jane is a very proper, well-spoken, attractive and gamine fifty-four-year-old lady. She was a drug addict for much of her adult life.

Some of the other addicts I know might be considered more 'hard core' than I. A very respectable businessman acquaintance of mine recently confided in me that he attacked somebody savagely, probably fatally, during a blackout. I was horrified to hear it at first, but then I've had blackouts many times and I've no idea what

I did during them. I could have done anything, so really we're no different.

On one occasion, I was on the ferry to England to meet a lover and I tried to throw myself off the boat. I had to be fished out of the sea by a life raft. I was as high as a kite. I can't rationalise what I was doing or why. The bizarre thing was I had gone to the trouble of putting on my new bikini for this watery end. You should have seen the state of me by the time I arrived in London: hungover, traumatised, confused and saying nothing. I never mentioned it. I spent the weekend with this charming man, drinking and drugging like I hadn't a care in the world.

My father died when I was eleven years old. My mother was a very naïve person, and didn't have any notion what I was up to. I was the only child. She was forty when I was born so she was like my grandmother in a way, two generations removed from me. She was terribly conservative and old-fashioned and I did the opposite to everything she said and did. If she admired something I was wearing, I took it off immediately. She never drank in her life.

I had my own daughter when I was twenty years old, the result of a drunken one-night stand. It turned out that there were consequences to being 'out of it' and how great this consequence. I couldn't believe it. I felt guilty that I didn't want the baby and I didn't want to be pregnant. I was so utterly useless myself. My family never knew anything about it, ever. My mother remarried when I was six months pregnant and I was at the wedding but she didn't spot my growing size.

I gave my baby up for adoption and I didn't speak about it to anyone for about fourteen years. My mother never suspected a thing, although I was in agony. I would say I was in mental pain for many years and I drank to dull and deaden that pain. My drinking took on a completely different bent. It was like desperation. I wanted to forget how life had happened for me, the way things were happening. When I was twenty-one I started doing drugs and I didn't look back for the next thirty years or so. Weed, magic mushrooms, acid, opium—it gave me wonderful dreams—and I liked speed, amphetamines and diet tablets.

But it was when I discovered cocaine that I was really in heaven. It became my absolute favourite drug. I used that as often as I could get it. I can't articulate just how much I loved it. The peculiar thing was, I had an elitist attitude towards certain drugs. I never touched a tranquilliser in my life. I had all manner of stuff up my nose, but I wouldn't take an anti-depressant or sleeping tablet or anything like that. I thought they were housewives' drugs. And I wasn't going to be a housewife.

I smoked dope all day every day. It was just part of my life. It was wonderful. The only negative thing I can recall is that I often went to sleep and missed the parties, passed out and missed all the action. But it lulled me. It made me feel numb and secure. One other thing that was kind of euphoric for me was that it seemed to open an extra ear to music. Music sounded fantastic when I was high and I could drift on it.

I had been in a long-term relationship with a man for many years and it ended badly when I was thirty-five. We were both drug abusers. Soon after the demise of our romance, I lost my house. Keeping up mortgage repayments hadn't seemed important to me at the time. The bank took my house back, but at the time I didn't care, I was completely in the throes of addiction, and anything concrete seemed complicated and tedious.

I moved to Wexford for a new life when I was thirty-six—very briefly full of renewed enthusiasm for making something of my sorry self—and I secured lots of different horticultural contracts. The plan was also to grow vegetables for sale to local restaurants. But I never saw the projects through. I never completed anything. I had a new boyfriend who was a very good gardener, so he made sure there was always lots of dope around, at the very least. I was using drugs daily now, anything I could get my hands on.

I didn't have the motivation to do anything much. Neither of us did. Our day began with a number of joints before we got out of bed in the morning, which set the tone for the rest. We would wander around, doing a little bit of gardening here and there, wander around for another little while killing some time, and maybe go down to Kilmore Quay in the evening and do the harder drugs until the small hours. Can you just imagine it, a crowd of middle-aged professional people who should have known better, doing all sorts of stuff, everything in fact, with the exception of heroin, every night of the week. Losers. We had no direction.

I was in Wexford, living this life, for a good few years and then I lost that house. Again, I hadn't bothered with the repayments and this bank finally caught up with me too. I hadn't thought about things like paying bills. I used to sit and cry in the house when the electricity was cut off: 'Why did they do this to me?' I couldn't understand why this was happening to me just because I hadn't paid a bill. I had no sense of responsibility whatsoever, and I was paranoid that 'they' were always against me.

I put all of these feelings of paranoia and helplessness and self-pity down to the drugs. I've discovered, since I've been clean, that I'm actually quite a precise and careful individual by nature. Since I stopped using, I always pay my bills on time.

I returned to Dublin just before my forty-third birthday and got a decent position as a housekeeper, cook and gardener for a 'good' and well-known family. But I messed it up. I was very high one particular day and I made a complete fool of myself and was asked to leave. It had become obvious—to them, never to me—that I had a drug problem.

I isolated myself at this stage, and moved out to Howth. I gardened out in Howth and lived in this beautiful cottage along the coast. I tried to kill myself some days. I swam out to sea a few times with the intention of killing myself. I think. One night I woke up on the floor of my bedroom, wet and wearing my bikini.

I still didn't think I had a problem. I thought I was one of life's poor unfortunates and would wonder why terrible and inexplicable things kept happening to me. I was drinking and using alone now. I was isolated, talking to the television, even spending evenings having arguments with the television, that sort of thing.

Then I let a very close friend down. It was coming up to Christmas and he said that we should meet for Mass on Christmas morning; it was important to him. I promised myself that I wouldn't use any drugs on Christmas Eve, because I really wanted to go to this Mass with him. To be there for him. But I let him down. I was so sick during Mass that I had to leave. I was sweating and shaking, and vomiting on the lawn outside the church and crouching on the ground. I realised that morning that I had no control and I stopped using drugs for a year.

Twelve clean and difficult months later—I was forty-seven years old now—I was working for a very well-to-do family and there was a lot of coke going around and I started using again. Instead of paying me my full fee by cheque, they would pay me half my fee in coke and half in cash, so I was off again. Once I had that first line, it was like I'd never been away from it. It was like seeing an old and fabulous friend.

I spent the next seven months using coke with this family, my employers, in very salubrious surroundings. Initially, I was delight-ed with myself. How I had fallen on my feet! But then months passed and I was on my knees. I wanted to die. The shocking mess I had made of things was staring me in the face every morning. I knew I was killing myself. And I wanted to live to one day meet my daughter. So I stopped. I left the family and I never used again. I threw myself into locating my little girl.

I did a mothers' course in Barnardos, which was fantastic. I met other women in my situation. I got on to the adoption agency and I have written a letter to my daughter. She hasn't replied to date, but I learned a year ago that I am a grandmother. I have a granddaughter who is three years old now. It's up to my daughter if she wants to contact me. My name is with the adoption agency, and they know that I'm open to it. I just have to leave it be now. It might happen. I don't like to get too hopeful because apparently, quite often, it's when an adopted daughter has a baby that she will look for her real mother, and that hasn't happened.

My own mother died a couple of years ago. She was senile and spent her last years in a home. After hating her for so long, I loved her then. I was so happy to be clean and to be available to her and to look after her. I'm so grateful that I got the opportunity to spend time with her. I really hope that she sensed how much I loved her. I think she did. We would hold hands and she would sing songs for hours on end. She died in my arms. I'm so very glad for those times. They are my lasting memories of her, of us together. And thank God for it. It could have been much worse. I feel I made my peace with her at least.

———

Julian is thirty-eight years old. Well known and instantly recognisable, he is impeccably well turned out in Dolce & Gabbana when we meet. This man doesn't have a hair cut, rather he has a hair 'style'. A journalist and regular TV contributor, over the last decade he has had a love affair with cocaine and is also a regular user of ketamine, 'a very powerful downer', Xanax, poppers, nitrous oxide, any pills that are going—'there's always a dodgy doctor around who will give you a script'—and alcohol in its many forms. Over the course of our lunch, two dealers call him on his mobile.

At Christmas last year, I was sitting in my parents' house for lunch— all of us gathered around the table—and we were talking about our fondest memories. Mine was a time about three or four years ago when I was really high and on the rip with my friends. My mother couldn't believe it. She spent an awful lot of time and money straightening me out and here I was looking back to her worst time as my best time. But it *was* amazing. We bonded and laughed and nothing mattered. I felt euphoric. I can still remember that feeling like it was yesterday.

Of course there have been dodgy times and dangers. I've often left parties on Shrewsbury Road at 5 a.m. to go to rancid flats in shitty parts of Sherriff Street in a taxi; the kind of places where you might reasonably expect to get shot, to meet the kind of people who you might reasonably expect to have a few guns. Inside cocaine would be wiped into dirty bags off a dirty table full of dirty people. A dealer will be anywhere in ten minutes if you're a regular customer, but sometimes I just couldn't stand around and wait.

I remember the first time I left my flat after I had come home having completed my time in treatment. My brother took me out for a dry lunch. We went to a pizza place in town; one of those restaurants where you can see the chef in the kitchen preparing the food. I was sitting facing the glass window the chef was working behind, and I was transfixed. I couldn't think straight. Every time he threw the dough in the air for the pizza base, flour would go everywhere. Clouds of flour puffing into the air. I was licking my lips and getting agitated gazing at it. It made me want coke so badly. We had to leave.

Both of my parents are upper middle-class Irish professionals. Not multi-millionaires, but certainly people of means. The people I hung around with as a teenager—all the other kids from the tennis club—were all big drinkers and pot smokers, so it was very normal to hang out by the beach to binge drink Friday, Saturday and Sunday night. Every week without fail. I robbed everything that could possibly be consumed from my parents' drinks cabinet, put it in a bag and said I was staying in a friend's house. The police would come every weekend and move us along the beach, but nothing ever came of it. We never got into any real trouble.

After school I went to college for a year to do economics and marketing, but dropped out, deciding instead to go to Austria skiing for a while. I had been skiing since I was four years old so I took a job teaching skiing on the slopes. I came back here [to Ireland], then moved to London to work on a very popular magazine, sourcing events and doing a social diary with Irish content. I earned the princely sum of £150 a week for that. My parents supported me because you can't live—certainly not where and the way I did any-way—for £150 a week in London. I dabbled a bit in drugs, just smoked dope, took the odd E-tab and did ketamine some weekends.

Back from London, I started working on a magazine here in Dublin. The party thing really kicked off when I was about twenty-four years old. My reason for starting to take drugs, and then for continuing and climbing the ladder to class-A drugs, was just greed. Nothing more. I have no deep-seated insecurities that I'm aware of. I was comfortable with my parents' divorce, and I'm equally comfortable with being gay. No. It was, and still is, just because I enjoy having a laugh. And I want to be having a bigger laugh than anyone else.

I was working as an editor now for a new publication here. They had approached me at a party. I was actually out of my head, having binged on coke for the first time ever, when a guy from the magazine approached me and asked if I'd like to be their social editor. I woke up the next morning and my head was a mess, but there was a business card in my pocket with 'Call Me', so I did, at about 2.30 p.m. He said, 'Come up to the office for an interview,' so I said, 'Okay, but it'll be later. I'm still in bed. How about 5 p.m.?' So I arrived for my interview in a tuxedo; I was on my way to an engagement party in Enniscree. I thought it was hilarious. I thought I should be offering *him* a job. He must have thought I was a right asshole.

Within the short space of about six months, I was doing coke every weekend; and by every weekend I mean from Wednesday lunchtime through to Sunday night. I was kicking off with a gram of coke, which would initially see me through a night, but then I'd have another bag the next day. I'd get it from a motorcycle courier-dealer. I'd been buying from him from the start. I had gotten his number, along with a few others, from colleagues of mine out that first night. I remember the first time I ever called, there was a code … You couldn't ever say the word coke or ask for it on the phone. I phoned up and asked for 'a couple of CDs'. And that's how he knew I was kosher, that I wasn't a new guy going to go to the police, because I had the inside track. I used to get it at lunchtime, the lunchtime of my working day, but my working day was so fluid and involved so many 'meetings' that I'd invariably be gone out of the office from noon and wrecked by 2.30 in the afternoon. I'd be taking coke through the evening until about two or three in the morning.

I'd go through at least a gram. Probably more. I'd be mouldy drunk at that stage also. It was very much a social thing. I certainly was never alone. The more my career grew, the more I was out, the more I had events and openings to attend. So the two—drugs and work—grew in tandem. The people I was with were all of a similar mindset and a similar lifestyle and had similar means, and I felt no different to them. It certainly never occurred to me that it might not be great for my career long-term that I be seen to be living this way.

There was a 'crew' of us at one point—at least ten of us, or so—that used to go to lunch four or five days a week, and I mean serious lunches; a couple of cases of champagne. Drugs were definitely a big part of our life and they were what we had in common. Where they were once a secondary part of our friendship, they had become the primary reason for us all meeting practically every day in the early afternoon.

There would be phone calls back and forth all morning while we organised who was bringing what today and where we would meet. We started having to vary our haunts, because dining in the same restaurants all the time was no longer an option. The staff came to know what we were at. We weren't exactly discreet. Restaurateurs in two of the places in the city had approached us about it and requested that we at least go to the toilet just one or two at a time. It looked bad. There would be five or six of us in the loos together, screaming and messing. 'Who cares?' You just don't care.

The people I was with had either media-type jobs or, more often than not, no jobs—they're just rich. So then every day, the battle of the egos would start about who was going to pay for everyone's lunch and the champagne. Who was the richest. Who could pay every day for a week. So there would be a chorus of people shouting 'Put it on mine! Put it on mine!' as platinum credit cards were flung around the table, landing in half-eaten desserts and on the floor. We were an odd bunch really, gay men and overly made-up women living off trust funds or wealthy men and varying in age from mid-twenties to late-forties.

Inevitably these lunches would roll on and before you knew it it'd be 6.30 p.m. and some event or other would be starting at seven. And I'd have had half plans to go and buy a shirt to change into, but sure fuck it, I wouldn't bother. I'd crack open another bag of coke to kill the time.

I would worry about how I looked, because so much of this lifestyle was about appearances and making an impression, but the irony is that the impression you're making is fucking atrocious because no matter what D&G suit you've just put on, you're off your fucking head and you're talking complete shite.

I remember one day in particular. We had been at lunch from about noon and had a huge concoction of drink and coke and then a few pills for the road washed down with a couple of cocktails before we drove to the Westin Hotel to this formal party. There were six of us in this Land Cruiser, which we insisted had to be parked at the front door. So a row ensued between myself and the doorman. Mid-row, I spotted a photographer who works for one of the broadsheets' weekend-diary pages and I stopped shouting to smile for him. I couldn't feel my face, I was almost hysterical at this stage abusing a hotel staff member, my suv was abandoned in the doorway, but I wasn't going to miss an opportunity to be photographed. Being seen in the paper in that state was better than not being seen at all.

I was working for a broadsheet now, which was certainly more than I deserved, but I never wanted to *do* anything. I was earning very good money but my parents were always supporting me too—paying for my place in town, things like that. I was having great times, out every night, getting free products and clothes; there was always a new phone, a new toy, a bigger party. I was given a free motorcycle and all I had to do was be seen around town on it, turn up at parties on it. So I did. I'd park it outside Lillies, in the laneway, and pick it up the following morning at seven and drive it home, out of my mind.

This was my life a few years ago; my career was soaring, I was in favour with everyone, there was a lot of media interest in me, all of these beautiful blonde girls wanted to go out with me, I was having such a buzz. The best time of my life. I got excited by free things, new things. Normal things like a dessert after a meal, a nice bottle of wine ... what? Those things were nothing. I wanted a crate of champagne before I'd condescend to attend a gathering. I expected to be given everything and wouldn't settle for any less.

That went on and on for quite a long time. I don't know for how long. It was a great lifestyle. Being paid to fly in and out of Ireland a couple of times a week. Off to the south of France for the weekend. I suppose the wheels were starting to come off in a way because, for example, I couldn't fly anywhere without doing a load of coke on the plane. I couldn't handle the boredom. As simple as that. Any flight longer than Dublin–London and I'd be in and out of the loo. I'd start to panic if I sat still. So I'd be feeling frantic, coked up to the eyeballs, drinking champagne, flicking through glossy magazines—flick, flick, flick—seeing nothing, turning pages, panicking and wearing dark glasses on a two-hour flight. I must have looked a right bloody mess, comical. I became impossible to please. If I was booked economy, I wouldn't get on the plane. I was being flown to Paris, for example, to work at a fashion show and I was being well paid for my work but I wouldn't get on the plane to get there unless I was in first class. Not even first class. It got to a stage where I wanted to be in seat 1A.

There were occasions where people would pull me up on my behaviour. In particular, I remember friends of my parents meeting me at a quite high-brow social event where I was off my tits and trying to have a word with me about how worried they were. I thought this was nonsense. I was only having a fucking laugh. What were they worried about? I remember telling them they should be worried about themselves because they were getting fucking old.

I was now spending far more on drugs than I was earning. When my parents lodged my allowance for my rent and various bills I would take it out and blow it on a massive lunch. So my rent on my house wasn't being paid; my belt started slipping. This was within six months of the start of the weekend coke use. My parents didn't know a thing. They don't live in Dublin so they didn't see a lot of me, although I'm sure they were hearing stories. Mum noticed that my weight was fluctuating when I did go to visit her and she would comment on it, but that was about it.

I started going into stores and taking all of the clothes that I wanted, announcing to the sales assistants that I wasn't going to pay for them but that I'd wear them to such-and-such an event or write about them in a magazine. Of course this was because I was in debt and all my income was going on drugs, but my lifestyle meant that having new and labelled high-fashion outfits to wear was a necessity. For somebody who was everyone's darling just months previously, I started to get snotty calls from expensive men's stores asking for their jeans back or for a credit card number. But I wasn't put off.

One day I walked into Brown Thomas and put on a Gucci suit in the dressing room, when my mobile rang. I was high as a kite and distracted by the call, so I walked out of the store on my phone and walked the length of Grafton Street in this suit and shirt, with tags hanging off it, no shoes or socks. I was at Stephen's Green looking in a jeweller's window when I realised I had no shoes on. I had no idea how I had gotten there. It took me about twenty minutes to recollect where I had come from. My mind was going. I had no concentration whatsoever.

Everything was turning grubby. My circle of friends was changing. I had moved 'up' a level where things were wilder, dirtier, later, longer. I was surrounded by flaky people like myself. Soon I was at parties that I wouldn't have been seen dead at previously. Nowhere glamorous. Crappy little house parties in shit parts of Dublin. I remember being utterly repulsed by it. The only thing that linked the whole group together was a massive bag of coke and ecstasy. And then it would be 7 a.m. and someone would be banging tunes until lunchtime. I'd be starting to come around at this stage, still drunk, but realising I didn't know where I was, and trying to get myself together to set about my journey home from some godforsaken place.

I had started inviting dodgy 'couriers' into the hotel where I was now living, at all hours of the day and night. I'd be at the main entrance in the lobby to greet them in a tracksuit and slippers.

I started having dealings with money lenders, guys at parties who trawl through the crowd looking for eejits like me to befriend. I had several unpleasant encounters paying back a Grant Mitchell look-a-like through his Merc's ridiculous blackened windows months later in the car park of the Stillorgan Shopping Centre. It was like *The Sopranos* meets *Desperate Housewives*. I mean, the ludicrous nature of it. 'Meet me at Nutgrove!'

I remember myself and a female work colleague ended up going out together one night. I suppose we were kind of seeing each other, briefly. I don't know what we did with the time, but we found ourselves in an early house the following morning, shaking and starving, wrecked looking, hiding from her fiancé. I rang a café near Ballsbridge and told them I was coming with a friend but had no money and we needed breakfast and alcohol. We found our way there and they gave us a bottle of champagne in a teapot because it was too early to serve us openly. I remember thinking how disgusting she looked. I considered bringing her to the hospital but I was struggling to keep myself together. Her phone kept ringing and ringing. We crawled from our breakfast to a bar for another few and then on to a restaurant, where we managed to lock ourselves in the loo. I had to ring the restaurant and say we were trapped in the toilet. Upon leaving the toilet, I bounded into the main dining area and knocked over a buffet table laid out for lunch.

Imagine it. I was wearing sunglasses, jeans and a hoodie, both of which were dirty and slept-in. I actually looked and dressed like a drug addict now (I had learned some time back to bring a hoodie out at night for covering a multitude and getting around without being spotted the next day). Worrying about my appearance was a thing of the past, and anyway, I wasn't being invited to as many high-brow events anymore. So there was a massive crash as platters of seafood, French toast and compotes and things hit the floor. And I and this girl thinking it was all hilarious. And still, when the manager asked us both to leave I was appalled and shocked. Not six months previously I was a regular daily diner at this establishment. I always got the table I wanted and there was champagne on ice waiting for me when I got to it. So of course I didn't go quietly. I argued and refused and insulted the staff and criticised the food.

I had forgotten that I had no money with me nor a credit card so it's probably as well we were thrown out when we were. I think she got herself into a taxi. All I knew was that she was gone minutes later. It was one of many totally fucked-up incidents. She was getting married, I am gay, we were having coke-fuelled sex at a crappy house party full of strangers and then trashing one of the best restaurants in the city.

Yet—is it bad to say this?—I loved it all. The madness of it all. I loved it then and when I recall it now, I love it all over again. I don't regret doing it. I regret what it did to me and to my work, but I loved being high. It had its downers, after … the feeling shit, but there was always another upper coming along soon afterwards. The fucking crack was unbelievable. Even though everything was crumbling around me, it was hilarious fun. A full-on non-stop party.

My work was really suffering now. I had three phones but was uncontactable on any of them. Work had become an afterthought, a petty annoyance in my life. I would come in on the last day of the month before the publications went to print and bang out something mediocre to fill the inches. The staff were tiring of me and my boss was getting on my back, losing patience with my attitude. I don't know why he even bothered trying to argue or reason with me. I was on another planet where I was the king. There had been rumblings of media interest in me from the UK, so my ego was at an all-time high. A UK station wanted me to take part in a documentary series about people with interesting lifestyles. This was right up my street. I'd get to be fabulous on UK television and everyone would see it. I didn't consider for a single second that there was a possibility that I'd appear even the slightest bit obnoxious, out of control, spoiled.

I remember telling my editor that the tables had turned, that I wouldn't be available to work anymore, that our roles had flipped and it was all about me, that I was carrying his paper now and not the other way around. All that had flipped was me.

So the UK production team flew me over first class, all of my demands were met, a car waiting for me, a stunning flat in Mayfair—everything I could have wanted. I was loving it. This was my life. This was what mattered and was real to me. So a camera crew followed me for a week, living my life with me. It was non-stop lunches, parties, launches and falling out of limos with models. I was well out of control and, to be honest, I don't even recall most of the week. I hadn't the sense to consider that everything was being filmed and that perhaps it might be wise to put my best foot forward.

There was nothing of substance, not even a flash of insight or honesty from me, which could have been filmed in the entire seven days. Of course, I thought I was getting on great with the crew. They were drinking with me, telling me I was wonderful TV and doing great, so my guard was totally down and I was living as usual, telling them everything, involving them in the whole adventure. In effect, over the week, I hung myself. I insulted everyone, babbling away, loving myself, high as a kite, being racist and hateful, lying my head off, and all on camera.

When it was broadcast, everything crashed and the nightmare started. I returned to Dublin and got abuse from every direction. I was really panicked, there was nowhere to hide, my parents would know, but I was still high as a kite. That night I did a tonne of coke and went to bed. The next day I was fired from all of my respective jobs and contracts—writing, editing, TV, etc. The phones were ringing all day. It was like the Twin Towers. Everything and everyone was gone. The landlord paid me a visit and told me to pack up. I was up to my eyes in debt and still sinking. It occurred to me that day, for the first time, that I might be a cocaine addict. I owed a scumbag dealer at least two grand that I had no hope of getting. I was in serious trouble.

Everything was a massive ordeal. I remember sitting on the edge of my bed crying, clothes all over the floor, utterly distressed because I couldn't decide what to wear. I had lost the basic skills of life and the ability to function, because my mind had been taken over by using coke, getting coke, hiding coke.

So I threw myself at my mother's feet and told her the whole story. I was hysterical and I started to cry like a baby. What the fuck had I done? I hadn't a single friend. Nobody, bullshit friends. I wanted my mother to put her arm around me and get me out of the mess I had made. Everything was on its arse. I had to make changes.

I went into a treatment clinic for a six-week stay. A beautiful place in northern Spain. It was the kind of centre where you could come and go, so I wasn't *entirely* clean for the duration but I felt better. I was surprised that I had managed at all really. So I left there and was back on the coke in no time. But I was taking less and things weren't so crazy. I was being watched by my family and friends. I couldn't afford another crash scenario like before. I got my life back in some kind of order, repaired some of the bridges I had burned, and I'm still managing to keep on top of things.

Now it's happening again. The interest in me is rising steadily, life is good, I'm getting free stuff again! And I'm ready. I'm more in control of it this time. I don't do drugs that much now. I'm not sworn off them by any means and I'm still living a very social lifestyle so I'm around them a lot. But there's simply no such thing as class-A drugs in this country. You're just snorting shite. If I do coke in any other country I wake up in the morning and I'm clear. Here, you wake up and there's filth up your nose. It's dirty and the quality is terrible.

There's no glamour in coke in Ireland: you chop it with a credit card and you snort it with a €50 note—that's where the 'glamour' begins and ends. Realistically you are kneeling on a piss-stained floor snorting dirty washing powder off a public toilet seat.

Chapter 7
The Arm of the Law

'I've just come out of my second stint in treatment for cocaine addiction. I feel like I'm losing the battle for my life. I can't conceive of a time when I'll ever feel "normal" again. I'm staying with my elderly parents now; I have their hearts broken—pathetic at my age. I've mixed feelings about ever returning to my job on the force now. I feel very bitter about the situations I've found myself in, the lack of training, the constant exposure to drugs. Maybe that's me not taking responsibility for myself, for my own actions, but that's how I feel. My life is in ruins. It's all I can do to get out of bed in the morning and spend the day fighting the constant urge to go out and score.'
GARDA C., AGED THIRTY-SEVEN

According to Detective Superintendent Barry O'Brien from the Garda National Drugs Unit, 'Gardaí who come into contact with drugs and work directly with drug seizures on a daily basis are not given any specific training with respect to the dangers, temptations or otherwise, and are not in any way briefed on how to deal with

spending their shifts in the company of massive quantities of illicit substances. There are no systems or procedures in place for this or for addiction awareness. The only safeguards relate to the guarding of the custody of drugs. That's about the best we can do to try to stop Gardaí drawing from this internal and available well.

It is very common practice within the Gardaí to turn a blind eye to addiction once someone is turning up for work, to steer clear of any level of confrontation. Sometimes, I wish people were less functioning or more obtuse when they're using because they'd get themselves into scrapes that couldn't be easily hidden or ignored. The organisation would be forced to confront them then.

When you talk about substance abuse within the Gardaí, you really have to include alcohol as well as illicit drugs, because there is a social 'culture' of drinking and winding down among the police force that goes back generations. It was and is a major problem within the Gardaí. I would say, as a profession, we are over-represented in terms of addiction. Generally drink and drug abuse in the Gardaí only comes to a head when there is some incident or other; not as a result of bad practice on the job usually, but rather, for example, being caught for drunk driving or causing a social nuisance.

The police force, just like any other section of society, will be broadly representative in terms of attitude and in terms of their practices, good and bad. We have probably always had an unfortunate relationship with alcohol. One of the key requirements of the police force is the regulation of the licence trade, so alcohol has always been readily available—the old anecdote about the Garda clearing out the pub and then having a few pints with the publican afterwards. There's also the element known colloquially as 'hawking' whereby people in the licence trade would be very happy to befriend the Garda and provide him with drink on tap. In effect, the regulating of the licence trade means that police officers have more access to alcohol than the next person.

The other element is custom and practice. Traditionally, police officers associate and socialise with other police officers. This is largely still the case. The majority of socialising among the police was, and is, in pubs; it's their epicentre. Also, I think the shift system contributes in a number of ways in that there are few places, other than the pub, open when you finish at 10 p.m. In addition, quite a lot of some Gardaí's work is actually conducted in pubs; they meet informants there.

The element of stress in policing is also a key factor in substance misuse. A lot of jobs are stressful these days, but there are particular times of acute stress when something happens and Gardaí feel they need an outlet. Let's say dealing with a big murder, where there are going to be many unsavoury elements; maybe attending the scene where the body is lying, attending the post-mortem which can be a very difficult experience, dealing with the family. In a lot of cases like that where you're working on an investigation, you'll be working eighteen-hour days, every day, at an acute level of stress and pressure. And the best reliever, for some, can be getting out of it.

Another very stressful time is during a major trial. I always say here that you know when there's a major trial coming up because there's an atmosphere about the place. Most people out there don't experience a trial. They don't experience their every action and move being forensically examined in a public forum. No matter how well an investigation is conducted there are always things at the trial that put pressure on the Gardaí involved and question their movements. They may spend a couple of hours being cross-examined and explaining their five minutes at the crime scene. Often the feature of the end of a trial is that people go off drinking. And it's doubtful that they'll have a glass of Guinness and go home. More likely, they'll spend the night there and God knows what'll go on.

So there's a whole host of factors. And then, we have had the same cultural ambivalence toward alcohol as the rest of society, despite being the policing element in it. Yes, it's true to say police officers were, and still are, over-represented in terms of substance abuse, relative to other professions.

In the police force, as in most of Irish society, you'll rarely hear someone say, 'He's an alcoholic.' You'll hear, 'He's fond of the drink' or 'He's a great man for the pints'. We couch our phrases to avoid using the term 'alcoholic' or 'addict'. You'd have to be in a treatment facility before someone would venture those words. I'm second-generation police. My father was a detective. He was the same rank as myself. All of his friends were police officers. There were many 'great drinkers' in his acquaintance.

It's very difficult to know that a Garda is an abuser of prescription drugs with any certainty, as the signs can be hard to pick up. But I will say that we have some of these in the force, because we are a microcosm of the larger world outside the station.

In relation to illicit drugs, I think the issue is a generational one. Widespread drug use has only taken hold in this country in the last twenty years, so in many ways it's in its infancy. It would mainly pertain to the younger Gardaí coming up through the force. We're not any different to what's going on outside in terms of drug abuse, and neither are our twenty- and thirty-something new recruits and officers.

Of course it's made more tricky because of the criminal law element. What do you do with a Garda who you know is a regular cocaine user, for example? It's not illegal to be a cocaine addict, but it is illegal to possess drugs. So if a colleague presents himself in front of me and admits to a drug problem and is looking for help, he hasn't broken the law. If I found him in possession, then he'd have a problem. That said, I have never had anybody walk into my office or seek out my company in this organisation to volunteer to me that they have a drug habit. And I think it is unlikely to ever happen. I would say that the catalyst always comes externally and it might then be pointed out to the person that he or she needs help.

It's a complex issue because we're the enforcers of the law and here are some of us breaking the law, and also because—due to the nature of our work—we have greater access to illicit drugs than anybody else, with the possible exception of drug dealers.

I think the fear of being found to have a drug problem is very acute among this profession as we are deemed to hold a certain responsibility. Similar perhaps to the medical profession. It's difficult for people with a position of extreme responsibility to admit to a vulnerability, particularly within an organisation that has a strong visible identity. Like the priest, a policeman is easily identifiable in the community as part of a group, so you're letting yourself down individually but also you're representing a wider, trusted unit.

In relation to illicit drug abuse, the inadequacy of the Gardaí lies in our lack of skills to deal with the problem among our own. It can often be purely a time management issue, whereby you mean to talk to someone, follow up with them, and suddenly you find four weeks have passed and you haven't found the time to do anything. We also tend to compartmentalise a problem. We come to a problem, we start the ball rolling for dealing with it, and we presume there is a solution at the end of the day. This is the culture of the police, to compartmentalise. But human beings don't fit into these neat boxes and neat timeframes and tidy resolutions. Also, addiction is for life. It's not going to be 'over' because the person did a few weeks in treatment. These problems can run and run for years, which is a struggle for the person and a struggle for the organisation.

Then there is the fact that officers may try to protect colleagues and shield them and their reputation. Because of the level of my position within the organisation, I only get a certain level of truth from Gardaí regarding members of the force who are using substances, but I think I'm quite sensitive to spotting someone with a problem. If and when I do spot it, I strenuously urge the individual to go for treatment, and I get on to the Garda Welfare Service to let them know there is someone requiring support. There needs to be consistency and follow-up afterwards.

I have great faith in Gardaí going for treatment, not because I believe it'll solve the problem but it's certainly a good place to start. When an officer goes for treatment, it's an acknowledgement that he has a problem that is out of control. Many of them go in not realising they need help, but by the time they come out they do. And hopefully they have a few more skills to bring to bear the next time they're in a difficult situation.

I would generally be against moving a Garda after treatment. He may see such a move as punitive and there's the danger too that you'll move him to a less sympathetic and foreign environment. It's like the area of clerical sex abuse; you move them from one area to another and give them a ripe, fresh playing field. I think it's preferable not to move the problem around. It's likely to never be mentioned again, however. We are not at the stage where it'll be openly referred to or discussed. We're not comfortable with that. The stigma is still there. Colleagues tend to take the view that— particularly when another officer has been away for treatment— their little problem has gone away now and everything is fine. Best not to dwell on it. Sure that person is no longer an addict . . .

———

Those in the legal profession face many problems, including negative public image, heavy caseloads, little time off, neglected family lives, difficult clients and unpaid services, deadlines and threats of malpractice. Like Gardaí, solicitors and barristers are susceptible to the same stresses and depression as the rest of us and some try to deal with it by abusing substances. They are quite capable of overlooking the law they've sworn to uphold.

Susan is a barrister. In her varied practice, many of the people she represents face charges of drug possession and drug-related offences. She has more in common with them than they might think.

I use cocaine every day now. It's an exhilarating high, but it's short, very short. Too soon I feel it wear off. I love the ritual and the thrill of anticipation, chopping and laying out the line and imagining the euphoria to come. But it's too short.

I use cocaine with my boyfriend at home, and also alone in my office at work. Quite a few of the people I represent are drug users, but not the successful kind; they're serious addicts and dealers. I feel like I could stop if I really tried, but there's a lot of pressure in this profession and I find that coke definitely makes it more manageable. It allows me to work hard, feel confident, be more accepting when I lose, and there's little or no risk of discovery. I don't worry about it. Why would I? It's just another part of my day-to-day life, like putting on my make-up.

———

'I bought my shirts in Dunnes Stores in order to keep as much money as possible for drugs. I'd say I was the only solicitor in the firm turning into the office in shirts that cost £6. I knew the price of everything and I was very careful about parting with money—unless it was for drugs or alcohol.'

Fintan is the middle child of a successful professional Irish family. All seven children are in middle-class professions and are addicts or recovering addicts. Despite being a legal professional, Fintan was never put off by the illegality of his drug abuse. In fact the criminal element never even occurred to him.

The family moved to a house he likens to 'Southfork', outside Dublin, when he was twelve. After a stint experimenting with solvents as a teenager, he started abusing substances when he was eighteen years old. A solicitor in a firm in Dublin's city centre, he now lives in south Dublin with his partner James. He sails and drives a classic car. His primary drug of choice was hash but he confesses that he would have used anything. He's still on antidepressants, but manages only to take them as prescribed. He is now forty-six and in recovery since February 2005.

I do think about using. Last Wednesday, I had a stinker of a cold and I got caught in the rain and was late for a meeting and a couple of other things went wrong and I thought to myself, well fuck it. Just fuck this day and sensible bloody living. I'd love to just go out there and get doped. But it passes. When I think it through I know that, for me, I might as well take a revolver to my head and shoot myself instead. It would be a lot quicker and less painful.

Addiction is everywhere. James and I are renovating a house in the country at the moment, and one of the leading workmen, who is very well known for his craft, is a big coke user. In fact, he has abandoned the project and taken off somewhere. For the last while, we've been looking for someone to finish what he started.

The reality of it is that only some people find recovery. A lot of kids and a lot of older people die. My sister-in-law died last August of an alcohol-related illness at forty-nine years of age. She's another middle-class statistic, and the death cert read cancer. She didn't have cancer. A lot of people just don't make it. They never find recovery, they never find any light and they die in darkness.

The middle classes who hit a wall with drugs, like me, have lots of support. Money can buy you therapy and help and treatment. Your peers have high expectations that you can recover, and that helps. They can see the light when you can't imagine it exists for you. The poor, inner-city guy doesn't have that. If he manages to establish some kind of sobriety and spells of being clean, he's considered a hero. That's not good enough. His peers aren't going to encourage him to get a job, to have ambition.

Both my parents were alcoholics and I grew up in a large, well-to-do family. My father was a heavy drinker, an alcoholic from as far back as I can remember. My mother, at a later stage, gave up on life and became reclusive and depressed and ultimately alcoholic too. I grew up in a family where communication was utterly non-existent, where feelings weren't talked about—a difficult place for a kid. You know, it was 'Ask your mother to pass the salt' and she would be sitting at the dinner table herself, or 'Ask your mother is she going to half-past-ten or half-past-eleven Mass'; this sort of thing.

I remember being embarrassed a lot as my father could arrive home drunk in the middle of the day and fall out of the car. I'd be mortified playing in the garden with my friends. I swore I'd never drink, I swore I'd never put any family, any wife, any person through the pain that we were going through. I hadn't yet realised that I had issues around sexuality. I didn't realise that I wasn't feeling towards girls the same way that other blokes growing up were. I went to a private boys secondary school and I was very unhappy. I performed well academically, but I was very low in myself and socially disastrous. My parents knew there was something wrong but nothing was ever said. They couldn't look after themselves, never mind take me on.

I was bright and I was willing, but things started falling apart for me from about age fifteen onwards. I became very nervous and I found life difficult. I had no one to confide in and I couldn't really share what was going on at home. Even though I had older brothers, I came from this family where feelings weren't talked about. I carried a lot of pain and secrecy and guilt and shame. I found being a kid really hard.

I started drinking regularly in my final year at school and when I left, at about seventeen, I took a job rather than go to college, because a job would afford me the wherewithal to drink. It was good fun. It made me forget my troubles. This went on for a couple of years.

My mother died when I was twenty years of age and very soon afterwards three of my brothers married. So there were big changes in a short space of time. Suddenly I was the only one at home looking after my father, my mother was dead, and the brothers and sister had moved out. Dad was still going strong. He was retired and had less money so he was more housebound, and he became dependent on medication rather than drink. Although he became seriously addicted to his pills, life was more stable and a bit more predictable because he wasn't falling in the door from the pub.

I was working and I started going to college at night to train to be a solicitor. I flew through exams and scored very highly, but I wasn't happy. I was having trouble with relationships and coming to terms with not being attracted to women. I couldn't really face or talk about issues of sexuality, although I was quite sure that there must have been other people like me. I was drawn to literature about sexuality and that kind of thing. But I still hadn't addressed it in any real way. I was drinking heavily and becoming more and more unhappy, living with the old man.

Blackouts were now commonplace for me and I started what's called 'controlled drinking'—trying to promise myself that I'd go home after three pints. But it never happened, because I couldn't. I was drinking at home alone too. My father's son.

I had fewer and fewer friends. I saw the situation I was in at home as being part of my problem. So I decided to move out. I answered a newspaper ad for a house-sharing arrangement with a lady in Terenure. It turned out that she was a drug user. Her husband worked abroad and was back only occasionally, so this house move was my introduction to regular drug use. She and I sat around smoking joints and snorting coke. It was just like home, only more dangerous. The luck of the draw.

My old friends would be, at best, occasional acquaintances at this stage. I'd started drinking with alcoholics I was working with whom I knew were prepared to go straight to the pub after work and stay until closing time. And now I had some using buddies too. I was really progressing up the substance-abuse ladder. I was using hash every day and was becoming increasingly depressed.

My father died some months later and I moved back home. My sister moved back from London and one of my brothers, who was in the Middle East, moved home with his wife and child. So there were three of us living in the house, all of us drinking heavily and using hash to get through the day, and me using coke to survive the evenings. It became even more like Southfork, in that people were moving in and out and bits of families were all living and fighting under the one roof. It was a big, grand house. One of my other brothers separated from his wife, sold his house and moved back in too. All of us were in various stages of active addiction to either drink or another drug.

In the meantime, I sat all my exams and qualified as a solicitor and was working in my first position, but not performing very well. I wasn't integrating with colleagues and my mind wasn't on the job. I'm sure I stuck out like a sore thumb among the others who were the enthusiastic young go-getting types that you would expect newly qualified professionals to be.

I came out when I was about twenty-seven years of age and moved in with the guy I had been seeing. However, the relationship really couldn't develop because I was high all of the time. I was using cannabis and indeed anything else that was available to me. Things were getting worse. The blackouts were worse and more frequent. I was now smoking joints and drinking in the morning, which is really a dead-end practice. The relationship didn't last, so I was back in Southfork again. At this stage, only one of my older brothers, an accountant, was living there. His marriage had recently broken down and he had lost his job, due to his addiction to cocaine. I too had no car, no job, no partner. I'd also been sacked some time previously. I suppose one of my many rock bottoms was around that time. As you can imagine, he and I were no good for each other, so I moved out by myself and into a flat in Rathmines.

I was trying to kick the drink, and managing okay because I was now smoking hash all day. It was 1990. My behaviour, without alcohol, was less erratic and within two years I had managed to get back on my feet. I was living in a house that I had bought in Drumcondra, paying my bills, working in a thriving legal practice in the area, and I was seeing a new man—a broker, James. After some months I moved into his house in Ranelagh. There was just the small matter of a now very serious drug addiction. Not that I admitted I was an addict.

I started attending AA meetings with James to keep me off alcohol. These made me feel very depressed about my drug use because I knew it wasn't a good idea. So anything I used from then on, I didn't even enjoy. It was masochistic in a way because I would beat myself up after using. I'd get very depressed and I'd swear again and again that I would stay away from it. But I would be back using every time, later that same day.

From 1993 up until 2004, I was using more than I can bear to admit even now. It was a constant battle, with short clean periods followed by days of bingeing. I reached a point were I really had had enough. I was very depressed and suicidal. I went downstairs one night late in December and I looked at the gas cooker and I wondered, 'If I turn on all the gas taps would that be enough to wipe me out?' I deliberated about this, sitting on the cold floor in the kitchen for a long time. But I thought about what James would face when he came down in the morning and something inside me told me I couldn't do it.

The following morning James found me still sitting on the floor in a worrying state. I don't remember this. He enrolled me in a hospital detox programme for ten days over Christmas. I went into residential treatment in the Rutland Centre when I was clean and I gave my all to it. Because I had ten years of AA under my belt, I had a fair idea what recovery was about. I came out of treatment in mid-February 2005 and I've been clean and sober since. I found it desperately difficult for the first six or seven months.

Very recently I've felt myself free of the absolute obsession to use. I've started to do things I enjoy, like sailing. James and I have been on holidays and there were no rows. I'm getting my confidence back and things are working out in my job. I've been so lucky—I landed a job with a fantastic commercial law firm. I met the managing partner through NA actually. He's been in recovery since 1991 and he gave me a chance. I'm much more integrated with people around me and things have just improved steadily since.

My boss obviously knows my history—as I know his—but I've told very few other people at work. I recognise a lot of people who are in difficulty from across a room. I see them in the office; other staff and clients who come in through the door.

I sleep like a baby at night, I eat well, I look after myself, and I go to the gym. Earlier this year, I bought a yacht—which was always a dream of mine. I went to Wales last month for a week and sailed the Menai Straits. Over the winter I did a yacht's master course and this weekend I'm doing a motorboat course. Life is out there to be lived and being in recovery allows me to do that. I love movies, and I'm mad about cars. I bought a classic car recently. I can't believe all that I've achieved since I got clean and started giving 100 per cent to my career. So much time I wasted before with my head filled with drugs and darkness. Two years ago, I couldn't imagine getting through the day. The future just didn't exist for me.

The rest of my family are all still in active addiction and struggling. Most of them are addicted to drink—I'm not sure if that is a good or a bad thing. Drugs seem to bring things to a head a bit quicker and dysfunctional drinking is far too easily tolerated in this country.

I have to watch myself because I have a great tendency to pill pop and I need to be careful about what I take. At the moment I'm on anti-depressants and I've been taking them only as prescribed. Hopefully I'll be off the medication later this year. I take that as it comes. I go to two or three NA meetings now each week. I think I'll always have to remind myself that I'm only an arm's length away from a drug on any given day. I have no doubt that if I were to stop going to meetings I wouldn't survive more than three or four months, and I would be either totally insane or in the thick of addiction again.

I think that most people who come into recovery feel they're too young or too old, or too educated or too wealthy. There's a lot of 'I'm not like them' and 'I'm from a good family' and that kind of thing. But really that's the disease talking. My disease is a cunning, baffling and powerful beast. It's the monkey on my back that I have to live with. It will find all sorts of ways to keep me from getting well and getting what I need. That's what I have to watch out for today and that's why I have to keep reminding myself how unbearable life was and easily could be again.

Chapter 8
Outside Hours

Garry is a forty-four-year-old pilot. He flies out of Dublin to various airports in the us at least a couple of times each week. He is a cocaine abuser.

I actually use coke more on the days that I am working and away than I do when I'm off at home. I find sitting still in the confined space of the cockpit for hours excruciating without it. I have to be very discreet—it's not something I want the cabin crew whispering about. I work different shifts and routes, spend overnights in the States quite a bit, and generally keep odd hours. I always seem to be packing and unpacking a bag.

Much of my time is spent alone and it can be quite lonely and boring; not at all how I imagined being a pilot when I was a young lad. I loved the idea of being in control of a powerful machine—there was something heroic about it. And of course seeing exotic places with gorgeous air hostesses! The truth is that aircraft largely fly themselves these days and, when we land, I tend to sit in front of the box by myself, doing coke, having a few drinks in a motel room and waiting for the morning.

I wouldn't say my cocaine use is out of control, no. It just keeps me going. I don't think my work is adversely affected by it. Nobody has ever said anything to me and, as I say, planes fly themselves. Unless you had a real and rare disaster.

———

When I meet Ultan, he is coming straight from an NA meeting. A forty-five-year-old divorced father of two, he now owns an acclaimed restaurant in the best part of the city centre, where he is also the Head Chef. Well-known in Dublin, he has a tremendous reputation as a talented chef both in this country and abroad. He is a recovering drug addict since 1996.

I used to really resent a good friend of mine, a doctor. He had this access to drugs, anything he wanted. I'd have literally swapped anyone, everyone, in my life for that. He used to go into the hospital pharmacy and say, 'Give me out 100 amps of morphine. I've got two sick cancer patients in Clontarf that I've to see tonight.' And then he'd go out to his car and shoot up. I envied him this so much, this ease. I thought he had it made.

But of course, if you're a doctor and you're shooting dope, you're not going to go buying drugs in the street with your mates. I think if you're from the inner city, you probably have a 'crew'. If you're living in a tenement block, you can be guaranteed that there are several other people in the building, if not on the same landing, who are in a similar situation. So there is camaraderie there. But business people like me and, even more so, professionals like doctors, are always really isolated. Even if they have access to every drug in the world. You can't tell anyone. Even if you suspect they're doing it too. It's a really lonely existence; you're totally cut off. There's no way a doctor was ever going to confide in his 'crew' at the hospital.

The old stereotype of the drug addict is some scumbag with

tattoos in an alleyway with a syringe having robbed a few purses. Drugs go with the film and music and modelling businesses, and somehow that's accepted. But much more so, drugs go with doctors, Gardaí and nurses—but we don't like to think about that. They're all susceptible. Especially because they have easy access to whatever they want. I think the spotlight should be shone on those dark corners. There's no class distinction, there's no boundaries with drugs, they're everywhere. It's not just an inner-city problem. It's the entire gamut of society, the whole rainbow of life. It doesn't matter how much or how little you have, or how strong or cool you think you are, if drugs want to get you, they'll get you.

When I was the Head Chef in one of the city's best-known restaurants, the owner would sell more coke and amphetamines on a Friday night to all the beautiful people seated in the restaurant dining area than he ever sold food. All of the white-collar professionals, men and women in power in Dublin, they were all there on Fridays to buy their drugs. There was a constant stream of people in and out of the kitchen and up and down to the office, buying their coke and pills and taking them then and there. Nobody was there for dinner. They all booked tables, but no one was there to eat. They just got stoned. These amazing plates of really fine, beautifully presented food sitting there going cold. No one even looked at it. The phone would be ringing off the hook for him from early evening until the small hours. He died last year. I consider myself very fortunate— blessed—to still be alive given what's gone on.

I grew up in a small town in the West of Ireland. My dad was a bank manager. He was a high achiever and had a major position in the community. He really was considered to be Somebody. Thirty-five years ago he was right up the ladder of Who's Who in the town—up there with the parish priest and the doctor. He was also a really heavy drinker. I was the second child and I saw a lot of violence in our home—my mum being beaten up and then he'd take it out on us. He beat us many times. There was a lot of shame attached to our family and I felt it. Despite being the bank manager's son.

I felt really unloved, different and isolated during my early years. By the time I got to thirteen, fourteen, fifteen and sixteen, I had arrested development. I hadn't matured like other kids. Emotionally, spiritually, mentally, physically, in every way, I was a dead duck in the water. I would never have been deep enough to question things, you know—Who am I? Why am I? What am I doing? How do I feel?

We moved to Dublin when I was sixteen. I was in school in Dublin for my Leaving Cert and there were a couple of kids in my class who were smoking hash and drinking cider at the weekends. I started smoking pot. It didn't really do anything for me, but I pretended, so that I could fit in with the rest of the gang. I really wanted to have a friend and to be a part of something. After about two or three months of that, every weekend I started to get stoned—really out of it. It gave me confidence, and it made me feel safe. I didn't feel fear. And in those early years of my life I was in a lot of fear. I was afraid of people, places, things. And when I looked to my parents, I thought: 'They're out of control. They're not going to be able to help me.' I didn't trust them. And that's where the isolation started.

In my child's mind I worked out that people weren't safe. So I didn't need them. I spent a lot of my childhood walking around the forests looking at the bluebells and the daisies. That's very sad. But that's the way it was. I was totally isolated from everybody else and I was in a lot of fear.

Some time later, I smoked the first joint that actually did work for me. Suddenly all those feelings disappeared. Instantly. I didn't wake up one morning and make a conscious decision to be an addict. I just didn't do that. Nobody does. Nobody wants to end up in a grotty lane somewhere with a dirty bottle of water, shooting up heroin that they bought off some dodgy guy. It doesn't work like that. Sure, there are people out there who can do drugs recreationally, but I'm not one of those people. We all start recreationally, but none of us knows whether or not we'll be able to maintain this, or whether or not we'll very quickly become an addict. It's a progression. I didn't wake up at thirty and say, 'I'm going to start shooting up heroin this morning. That's what my life needs.' It's a progression. And you can't see it when you're living it.

So I started smoking hash. By the time I got to eighteen and nineteen, I had absolutely no social skills whatsoever, I had no idea what I was going to do, and I had no Leaving Cert—I had fucked that up. I was under a lot of pressure from my parents. My dad was institutionalised in St John of God for his alcoholism. He was forty-four years old and he had been kicked out of his job. Here was this high achiever enjoying a great career, but his drink and his pills caught up with him. He was confronted by his boss because he was considered to be a loose cannon, he had a mental breakdown, and he ended up in St John of God. The bank put a pencil through his name, his career, and told him, 'It's over. You're finished.'

I would have spent all my time at twenty-one, twenty-two, twenty-three in this very room here *[we are in a very popular bistro-pub off Grafton Street]*. I started taking LSD, amphetamines, and steadily made my way up the drug food chain. And then I found cocaine. Cocaine is seen to be sexy and it's cool. It's like a good Marlboro ad. People associate it with wealth and everything that's going on in Ireland here today. It's wealthy out there. Ireland is a great market for drugs—the backdoor into Europe. It's big money and that's why it's dangerous. I was out buying drugs once, and there was a guy in the queue ahead of me and maybe he was having a bad day, but for whatever reason, he had a knife on him and suddenly all hell broke loose. There was nothing sexy or glamorous about that. Drugs, and the people they introduce you to, are bad news.

And then I found heroin. I smoked my first heroin in a really nice, stylish pub around here. I'd go into the bathroom and smoke heroin. It was going on all around me, and it was at a time when there were only a few people in Ireland in the drug squad. And suddenly there was a bumper crop of heroin abroad and it made its way here. Europe was flooded with heroin in the 1980s. It was £5 for a small bag at the time. It was shit, cheap heroin. For about six months after that I smoked heroin regularly—every weekend. On Fridays we'd get a quarter between three of us and we'd split it up, and get stoned. But then suddenly I was looking for it on a Saturday night and on a Sunday evening—sitting at home with a bag to improve my evening. Then the weekend was starting on a Thursday, at lunchtime. At 1 a.m. I'd be totally high. I was already a social misfit, but it was really turning me in on myself more deeply, not bringing me out of myself as you might expect. I couldn't communicate with anyone at this stage, but in a way that suited me fine.

And after about four weeks using it that often, I was actually physically addicted to it. I'd wake up in the morning and I'd be sick. My body was in pain. It was an obsession of the mind for sure, and a sickness of the soul, but also physically I needed it. It's a painkiller—a major painkiller—but I didn't know that. I didn't know what I was doing. All I knew was that when I smoked it, all of the pain was gone. I was in a euphoric state, a cocoon of really great and safe feelings. I felt bulletproof and strong and confident. But as soon as the drug was taken away from me for even one full day, I started to get sick. I'd go back out again to buy some more. So as the days and weeks and months went by, the £10 bag that we used to share had become a gram to myself—which was £100— and now it was daily use. Every day. It had to be. So a gram a day— that was a lot of money for a young man. I was holding down a job and I'd buy five grams, so I'd sell four of them and have one for myself. I was selling them among a circle of people that I knew.

I was getting mine from a bigger dealer down the line. Here's an example of how the dealer chain works: I lived in London for six years and I had a great job in an amazing restaurant in the middle of Kensington. Everyone who was anyone dined there. Lady Di was a regular. I lived in Brixton. I had a dealer whom I went to every day and he was getting his supply from a Nigerian guy—a clean-cut black guy called Mike, who had the sense not to use drugs himself. Suddenly I was moving in another world. I wasn't in the normal world. I was moving in an underworld—involved in something very illegal and in a place that was dark and sinister and mysterious. I was networking and meeting people who would be useful to me, for drugs.

So this dealer's name was Harvey, and I knew that if Harvey didn't have something, then this other guy in Stockwell would, ten minutes down the train track. I built up a network of telephone numbers of dealers. But it's all mercenary. They're not friends. If push came to shove, you'd be shoved in a heartbeat.

When an addict is desperate enough to get his fix, he'll do and say whatever it takes. And if that means cycling around with a lump hammer ready to bash someone over the head for a handbag, or going into work and pulling out the last cheque of the cheque book, or swiping a credit card belonging to a customer—you've got to do it. Come hell or high water. If your wife has €1,000 in her handbag, then you're going to take €500 and go back later for the other €500—but you'll swear you didn't.

So I was in my twenties—twenty-six or so—and I hadn't really got into any trouble or anything yet. I had a cool apartment and a great job. At this time I was just smoking heroin. I wasn't injecting it. So I had no marks. I had worked out in my head that injecting was hard core and that wasn't for me. I had seen people doing it. I was happy to get stoned by smoking it. It was clean and there were no visible signs on my body, no holes in my arms. It seemed to be manageable. I could go into the toilet at work at 5 p.m., smoke some heroin, put my tinfoil away and go in and do eight hours of work, ten hours of work—I was like Superman. I felt it increased my performance, but when I look back it was just an illusion. If I saw a video of myself from then, out of my head and cooking for mega-stars, I'd see that I was just not there. When you're out of your head you're just that: Out of your head. If you were out of your head and driving a car, you'd be out of control. It was like that. I was out of control.

So one day I walked into work at 5 p.m. to get ready for that evening, and my boss, Jonah, a great guy, was sitting upstairs in the dining room. He was waiting for me. He confronted me, saying he knew I had a drug problem and he was there for me. He offered to pay for a treatment centre for me. One of his friends had had a problem and had gone to this chi-chi place in London. Money was no object. He knew that I was good and he wanted to hold on to me. So here was this golden opportunity for me. I just panicked. I said I'd think about it. Here I was being confronted for the first time in my life. For the first time, someone called me on my shit and wanted to help me. Up until that, I had been self-will run riot. I was ducking and diving with drugs and working and making a lot of money. So I had this great job, an amazing apartment, a beautiful girlfriend, a great couch, a fish tank, fancy holidays (travelling with drugs in my bag). I moved in this very moneyed circle. On the outside it all looked bloody good.

My girlfriend knew about it, but we both played along with the lie. Obviously when one person in a couple is using drugs any chance of a healthy relationship goes out the window. We barely had sex. I just got really high all of the time. Eventually she left. She got really tired of the lying. Because when you're using you lie all of the time. It's a full-time job when you're an addict. It really is.

I'd go from Kensington to South London in the early afternoon to score during my break between the morning and the evening shifts at work. It would be a two-hour round trip on the train. If I went in a car it could have taken much of the day. So I'd get down there and make the call. There were very few mobile phones then. So I was relying on calls all of the time. And then when I'd finally make contact, it might be a hard luck story—'I've nothing. You'll have to wait until 5 p.m.' I was constantly under pressure to get my drugs, to make the money to get my drugs, to get to work, to make the calls, to maintain my lifestyle. I had a great income but I never got a full pay packet. I'd be getting subs each day to pay for my stuff. So by the time Friday came each week, my pay packet was a shadow of what it should have been.

It's a horrible existence. It's a really isolated existence. Who can you tell? You're on your own. The only people you've got are this circle of deviant friends who are living on the wrong side of the tracks. I couldn't relate to them. I had grown up in a place where people took pride in their surroundings and their appearances and had good manners. I was still like that then. But now I was going to see these young punks from Scotland living in a ghetto in London; living like animals. They had nothing, living in dirt with their babies, shooting dope out of cans.

So Jonah confronted me that afternoon, and I panicked. Now I wasn't on my own. He was a friend and he wanted to help. I muttered something about thinking about it through my cold sweat. A couple of days later, I was out buying drugs and driving through the city off my head when a policeman stepped out to stop me. I just kept going. I couldn't think clearly, and I'd a bunch of dodgy people in the car. I nearly killed the policeman. So I was arrested for that. I got locked up for the day, I missed a day at work and then the police came around to check that the restaurant was my place of work. The cake was starting to crumble. I felt like I had to leave London. I couldn't handle it any more. With the police and Jonah, the spotlight was on me. Me: the head chef at one of the most prestigious restaurants in the city. It was heavy shit.

So I left London, and came home and settled into life in Dublin. I was buying within two days. And then I turned a corner, a very dark corner. I started shooting up. I was in my parents' house one day and my sister was there. She's a nurse. She had left some syringes in a basket in the bathroom, so I picked one up and I just took it. The day I took that syringe, I happened to have cocaine on me. So I shot that up. And I was really fucking stoned. I thought, 'This is much better. I'm going to need a little bit less and I'm going to get a bigger buzz.'

So it all went downhill from there. I started to get more and more fucked up. I'd get great jobs, but I'd fuck up after a while. And then I'd get another one. By the time I was thirty-four years old, I was running out of options. I had this bizarre existence, whereby I was the Head Chef at one of the most renowned restaurants in Dublin and yet I was homeless. I had been living in an apartment in Temple Bar but I hadn't paid my rent in six months. I couldn't keep track of bills or get it together sufficiently to be organised about things. So I got evicted. I was on the street.

I think my family knew—or had a very strong suspicion—about my problem for a long time. I used to post home blocks of heroin from London to my parents' house during my time there, so that when I'd come back to Dublin for a week now and again I wouldn't have to go looking. Our lifelong postman would deliver these bricks, badly wrapped in brown paper with stamps all over them, to the fucking house. I'd sit up in my childhood bedroom for the entire week I was home with my tinfoil, smoking heroin. Of course my parents must have known. They found my paraphernalia all over the house. It was never talked about. They didn't know how to deal with it. Drugs were something that people from bad areas did. They were the ostriches with their heads in the sand.

I got to a place where I was having a mental breakdown. I was having panic attacks, I couldn't go out, I couldn't speak to anyone. I lost it. I had a great reputation in the city, I knew all the movers and shakers—I still do—and I was hiding from life in my single bed in my parents' house.

My last uses were incredibly dangerous. I was shooting cocaine. Think about it, a gram of cocaine. Snorting a quarter of a gram that's any way decent would get you high as a kite. But I'd be shooting it into my arm and then two minutes later refilling the syringe. At any one time I'd have a gram of cocaine floating around in my system within a period of twenty minutes. I was building up a tolerance to it. But any of those times another single grain could have killed me.

My last use was sitting in a bath, on my own, in my parents' house, trying to find a vein in my dick to shoot into because I'd no veins left anywhere else. Nearly thirty-five years of age, hiding in my parents' house because people were after me—serious people were looking for me—because I'd ripped them off and stolen their drugs. How great is that?

Emotionally, physically, mentally, spiritually, financially, I was bankrupt. I had hit a brick wall. I knew I needed help, that I needed to detox. So I dragged myself to Jervis Street Hospital and signed on a methadone programme. I didn't know what else to do. This was the only place I could think of to go. The methadone scripts gave me a brief respite from other drugs; I wasn't under pressure to buy every day.

Eventually I told my sister, the nurse, and she came with me one day to this detox programme I was trying. She met the doctor. This one doctor had taken an interest in me—I suppose I stood out there among the kids from Buckingham Street flats. There weren't many old guys like me from good families choosing to sign up to a methadone programme in Jervis Street. I mean, the place was dangerous. Full of people I would never relate to. I was more isolated than ever in there. I felt like I was taking my life in my hands. I was living in fear going down there, just getting my detox.

This doctor said I really needed to be in treatment. He got me an interview in the Rutland Centre. I didn't want to go but my sister made me. I was told not to use any drugs or drink before the interview. But I drank a bottle of brandy standing in the hall before I got into the car with her, so I turned up at the Rutland out of my head. The counsellor who assessed me told me I was a serious drug addict and that if I kept on the way I was going I'd be dead by the time I was thirty-five. I was only two months shy of thirty-five. But it didn't matter to me. I was full of arrogance and ego. In reality, I was actually terrified. I was a man but I couldn't feel anything. I wasn't a man at all, I suppose, just a ball of fear. I couldn't find my way back. I couldn't even conceive of ever joining the normal human race again. I wouldn't be let in.

I got into the Rutland four weeks later. I knew nothing about it. I didn't know what I was in for. It was blind faith and utter desperation. I went to the Rutland and I was 'clean', in so far as I hadn't used drugs in a month. That was the condition of entry. Clean, drug-free urine. But I was drinking constantly to try to make up for the drugs. I was in a pub on Townsend Street at seven o'clock having a tonne of gin and tonics the morning that I was admitted.

It was a six-week entry and, after about four weeks in this group with seven people and two counsellors, they told me I was wasting their time and that they were sending me home because they couldn't work with me. I had just been sitting there, drunk, rocking back and forth, saying nothing. I didn't understand what they were trying to get out of me. I started crying when they told me they were sending me home. I just broke down. I cried and cried and cried. I don't think I ever cried before in my life. Ever. It just wasn't a part of me. And that, I suppose, was a turning point for me, as simple as it sounds. Or as irrelevant as it might seem to you. They probably weren't going to throw me out at all. They were just trying to put pressure on me to get to a place where I had to want help. I couldn't take this final rejection. I couldn't bear that they were turning their backs on me because they thought I was a waste of space. But it wasn't a game. I was fighting for my life. I see that today.

After four weeks in the Rutland, I was introduced to a doctor— an addict himself. He was about ten years older than me and wearing a tweed suit and a tweed hat. He was the very first person I ever actually identified with in my life. He had been an addict himself and he was talking about drugs and, whatever he said, he told my story to the group. Word for word. It was like he was describing me and my life. I was drifting in and out of his spiel, but it was uncanny. When I listened to him, I heard my story and I could hear that I had a problem and I admitted to myself, and to him, that I was an addict.

So I did my treatment. And the day that I left there I had two choices. I had no choices while I was in there. But now I was out, and I could either go to meetings and stay clean or I could go back out and pick up where I had left off, which would have been the process of killing myself. Picking up where I left off would have meant going straight to an alleyway with a bag of drugs and some tinfoil. It would have been only a matter of weeks before I was dead.

Things were very different when I came out. I didn't get all cerebral about it and question it and think 'This isn't likely to work.' I was so full of fear that I didn't even question it. I just went to meetings. I didn't think about it. I just went. I was like a robot. All I did was go to meetings and sit there. I didn't talk or 'share' but I felt I had to be in a room surrounded by people like me.

There were six of us at the first NA meeting that I attended. Two of them are really well known in Dublin today for their professions. One of them is a furniture designer and one a diplomat. There was also a dentist and two businessmen. They were all educated and very middle class, well-to-do, wearing nice clothes. I sat looking down, so all I saw was their shoes—good shoes. They all looked happy and healthy, they smelt nice, and they were from the same neighbourhood as me. They were like me. Middle-class, white-collar Dublin. I felt really fortunate that they were there.

I still go to meetings, several meetings a week. It works for me. It's not for everyone though. There are other people who go up a mountain in Bratislava and chant, you know. But that's not for me. I'm never going to levitate. I'm just not that kind of guy!

When you're using drugs, it takes up all your mental time. I'd go to work in the morning and I'd be thinking about drugs. I'd have taken some before I went to work, just to get me through until lunchtime. I'd be thinking in work, 'I need to get money to get the drugs,' and then I'd make a few calls at work to see if anyone else wanted to go in on buying some. Maybe I'd buy half an ounce and sell a couple of people a gram each, and then I'd have to set up the meeting for during my lunch break. By two o'clock, I'd have my dopes lined up and work would be quiet for a while. I'd get the money, go and buy it, take some, meet the other people, split it up, get mine, get going, and take it again. It's an exhausting business. It's not like you're going to buy a bottle of whiskey. It's illegal, so even though it's readily available, it forces you to be constantly on the move.

Of course, it's not all illegal. There are a lot of people in their homes eating prescription drugs by the handful too. There are tonnes of people heavily reliant on very addictive prescription drugs. I know several high-class women myself who utterly depend upon Valium, Xanax and other anti-depressants—eating them like Smarties in their Shaker kitchens.

A friend of mine, aged thirty-nine, has two kids and is married to a very successful businessman who owns half of Dublin, but who's never home. I know she has days where she sits in the closet in her bedroom swallowing a dozen pills with Jack Daniels just so she can steady herself sufficiently to leave the house and attend a lunch.

Chefs are vulnerable to the party lifestyle. It is a high-pressure job, if you're in a top restaurant. It's very stressful, and you've people coming into the kitchen to meet you, like a celebrity. And sure, there's a lot of drugs. Chefs live outside the nine-to-five norm. We inhabit an 'other' world to begin with. We come out of work and it's the middle of the night. The party is in full swing. You're straight to a nightclub if you want a beer with a friend. Some people like that world. You're working in a kitchen, and then leaving there and it's the middle of the night and within minutes you're in a heaving bar. It doesn't compare to the guy going for a glass of Chardonnay and a sandwich at 6 p.m., before heading off home. Chefs walk out of work and into a party. And people might know you if you've a reputation around town because of your work, and you want to be part of the party, and the party people want you at their party. No better way to forget about the day than to get fucked up, stay in bed until 1 p.m. the next day and go into work in the afternoon. The hours lend themselves to that life.

I went to a staff party two weeks ago and there was more cocaine at it than I had ever seen in my whole life. There were five different types of coke. 'This guy has Number one at this table and this guy has . . .' It was almost like a joke. The quality is much better now and it's so open. There's always the split at any party: the coke crew and the no-coke crew. The party within the party; the group that will be in the bathroom or out in the garage or down in the back living room. And the mirror out on the table and bags of cocaine everywhere. Look at what's been taken off the streets. The other day, the police seized 15 kilos worth of heroin. When I was doing it a decade ago, you wouldn't have got 15 kilos worth in a year.

Someone who's using hard drugs three or four times a week to get through their work? They have a problem. They're addicted. Normal people go to bed, get up an hour earlier, drink four strong coffees and get their work done. That's normal. The illusion people have with drugs is that they're in control of the drug, not the other way around.

You can be a father and a husband and do your job and see your friends. We're all capable of doing all of our roles, and more. We can do it, without drugs. When you're doing drugs, your mind isn't on the job—you're impaired.

Please God my children never go the route I did. I feel so fortunate to be here and to have children. I'd be very sad for them because it's such a miserable and terrible existence. It's shocking. It brings you to a lot of dark places and it robs you of your dignity. I try to be a good parent. I do my best with it. They know I'm in recovery. They've been to meetings with me. After one recently, my seven-year-old daughter asked: 'Daddy, why did you tell those people you're a drug addict?' And I said: 'Because I am, Molly. That's the way it is. Drugs are bad.' But I minimise it for now. They're children; they have no comprehension.

Cocaine is definitely the drug of the moment, but heroin is still out there. It'll re-emerge onto the scene with a bang to claim its market in affluent Ireland. When I was doing heroin, it was a dirty drug. Nobody wanted to know about it. We were all middle class, but heroin wasn't. I know a number of very chic and sophisticated people whom I meet around the city and who come into my restaurant now and are using heroin to supplement their coke use. I'd love to glamorise it and say there were times when there were suitcases of money in my hallway and bags of drugs lined up in my lounge, but that's not how it is.

People who use coke a lot are often really well read and impressive because they're up all night and they're on the internet or they're taking things in and they're reading, reading, reading; they're busy. Cocaine keeps you up and busy. You could fight a war, and bake a soufflé and fuck your wife and drink two bottles of wine and mow the lawn. There's a great example in that movie *Goodfellas* where Ray Liotta is making a cake, and cooking pasta, and smuggling drugs and he's killing people; he's got it all going on, and it can seem like that. That's how you feel. But it's not reality.

———

Hannah is a classical musician with one of the country's leading orchestras. She performs regularly at lunchtime recitals and evening concerts. She has been taking the cardiac medication— beta blockers—to control stage fright for the last nine years.

The mornings of a performance I will wake up jittery and panicking. I'll feel sweaty and nauseous at the prospect of playing, even after all these years. I'll take a few—a handful, I suppose—of pills and I'll feel more in control of my body. I haven't performed in public without beta blockers in nearly a decade. I wouldn't be able to. They calm me down, stop my heart from pounding out of my chest and me sweating through my clothes. I often perform difficult solos and I couldn't trust my hands to do what they should without them.

I take as many as I need during the day and through the evening, and maybe a handful before I go on and during the interval that night. I'm not the only one. They're thrown about like Tic Tacs in the Green Room. One of the other musicians is married to a doctor, so there's never any problem with prescriptions or getting them. I try not to take them on days when I'm off, although it has happened. I haven't had any side-effects really. Sometimes I'd feel a bit weak soon after taking them, or the next morning I'd feel a bit on edge, but it's far preferable to the alternative, which is freezing in a pool of my own sweat in front of 500 silent music lovers on a Friday night.

What would I do if they were taken away? I'd have to teach school children to play the violin in my sitting room for a living.

————

Karl is a columnist for a national publication and is a popular media figure. He uses cocaine at least three times a week. He claims it is the only way that he can get his columns and features

finished on time. In his mid-50s now, he has been using drugs for nearly four decades.

I love what I do. I love journalism and getting a reaction to what I write. After I graduated from Trinity, I worked as a theatre actor for about nine years. I've performed in the Abbey, the Gate and the Peacock and in the Lyric in Belfast with various theatre companies. Over time, I got involved in script writing and then made the move to journalism. And that's what I've been doing for the last twenty years.

I do about a €100 bag of cocaine over the course of a day, maybe three times a week, particularly in advance of a big deadline. I find it helps the efficiency of my train of thought. I'll write profusely through the night and I'm usually happy with the result. Maybe I'm getting a little soft in my dotage and need to keep my edge this way.

I have had bleaker times where I've sat at home alone methodically going through three grams of coke and doing little else, but that was when things had got out of hand in the mid-1990s. The quality of my work suffered during that period, although the quantity probably tripled. Most of my writing was just shockingly rambling and had to be heavily edited in-house. Apparently I was a total dickhead as well and said wildly provocative things. Well, so my nearest and dearest assure me! I think it shone a torch into the darkest corners of my mind and erased any commonsense filter between what I thought and what I said.

Although I enjoy my life, if my nephew or niece were to replicate the lifestyle that I have, I wouldn't be happy about it. I'd be pissed off in fact, very much so. I wouldn't think that there are very many healthy people using drugs on a consistent basis over time, like I do. Many of my media colleagues use drugs recreationally, and I suspect a good number use a lot more than that, but not the ones that are well-adjusted and content and healthy. Am I saying I'm not well-adjusted and balanced? Yes, I suppose so.

At times in the past I've certainly found myself in company that I would never have chosen, were it not for the fact that this person could supply me with what I needed. I'd then feel the need to hang around and have a drink with them to be polite, because my mother brought me up that way. To be respectful to others in our society! Of course, she also told me not to sleep around or take drugs . . .

When I was young I started taking marijuana, mushrooms and acid, that kind of stuff. For me, it was certainly a rebellious move then, pushing things a step further than smoking. I enjoyed it. I wanted to be controversial, at home, at college, in the theatre. Very quickly I ended up feeling compulsively drawn to it. I remember clearly the first time I saw someone in my company take cocaine. I was seventeen and it was in a house in rural Ireland. I was unreservedly shocked, but equally fascinated. Cocaine in 1971 in a bungalow in the midlands! I didn't start taking coke myself until many years later, when I was about thirty-six. I got into trouble with it quite soon afterwards, but then managed to regain control of the amount I use. I've been using it on and off for the last twenty years or so.

For the last seven of these twenty years, I've given it up for one month in the year and as I'm coming to the end of the month my mind is very clear, although I think I'm less productive in terms of output. I'll have a few days reflecting on the bigger picture and mentally shuttling through the previous months and years and decades. Usually, I'll conclude that getting involved with drugs was perhaps one of the greatest mistakes of my life, but I still start using again—with the same frequency as before—just as the first day of the new month dawns. I can't seem to break this cycle. I'm not much of a drinker. I find alcohol messy and it adversely affects my work too much. I suppose there's no real pressure on me not to use drugs either from my family or from an employer. I work from home on my own hours and my wife tends not to comment on it.

At this stage of my life I'm not too concerned about friends or work colleagues 'discovering' I still use drugs. My use is done privately, at home and alone. I buy my own and I don't share. I'm not a party-goer or a particularly social animal and never have been. I don't lobby for their legalisation and I don't think I influence anyone else's opinion. My long-term supplier got busted recently, but he vouched for me to a friend of his. Although there are drugs everywhere in media circles, small-time dealers can be a bit wary of making a drop to a known journalist.

Definitely my life has been affected by drugs. If I had led a cleaner life, I'm sure I'd have had smoother relationships. Maybe I'd have married earlier, and maybe I'd even be a parent. Yes, I think I've been playing catch-up in my personal life because of drugs. When I was a younger man, there was certainly a lot of time wasted. But I'm settled now and I accept my lot, and I'm almost comfortable with my fairly manageable dependency.

Interestingly, there are only two other people in my extended family with dependency issues and the three of us share the same Christian name. I muse upon that from time to time.

Fiona is a scriptwriter and film director. She lives in London since June of last year, having 'diddled' her bank in Dublin to pay for her cocaine habit. At thirty, she had done some great film work; had the promise of a movie deal, was at the top of her game in Ireland, and had no debt. 'Recreational' drug use took over and now, six years later, that impressive career trajectory has not continued. She is considered difficult and offensive by many in the film industry and has built up massive debt despite maintaining a more than healthy income. 'Financially, I'm a mess. That's not to say that I regret those extreme years; I mean, I'd never swap them for a stable job in IT,' she says. Fiona is now thirty-seven and still using drugs, albeit to a lesser degree.

I left Ireland last year; there was too much to face up to, too many people I had upset and too many relationships—romantic, professional and financial—that I had soured and that I can't ever repair.

I remember the sheer sense of elation the first time I did coke. I was about twenty-eight, a late starter really for my peer group. My supplier had chopped out two lines on a small mirror, one for each nostril. I did them together. The rush came on almost immediately. I felt great. The drug definitely lived up to all the hype. I resolved to become a regular user from that night on.

It was the late 1990s, my career had taken off rapidly and it showed no signs of slowing. I was working a lot. I had contracts with various production companies and with a big film channel in the UK. I had no concept of tax or balancing my accounts or any of that. It was very much a freelancer's lifestyle: cheques coming in, getting cashed, waiting to be paid for a big contract, ignoring bills until I got a final demand and so on. I had just broken up with a long-term partner and was living it up, spending a fortune on alcohol and now drugs too, and eating out. I'd very quickly have periods of no money where I'd have bought coke and pills with whatever cheque arrived in the morning post, but never thought to fill the fridge. I'd come back from paid first-class flights having met with film companies in the UK or the US and find myself desperately searching down the back of the couch for enough coins to buy a pint of milk.

I've always had very easy access to whatever drugs I want and more, due to the circles I move in for work. I've never had to look for drugs or go to any lengths to pick them up, or—sometimes—even to pay for them. In my absolute worst-case scenario, cocaine was only ever thirty minutes away—£100 a gram at that time, including delivery.

In 2000 I got a call from a guy in prison—serving time for a gangland killing—who wanted me to visit him with a view to writing his story and seeing the screenplay made into a film. I had interviewed some of his 'friends' for various documentaries previously. He was thirty-two, only a couple of years older than me. He told me about his life and his trial, about the gang and his betrayal of his father. It was a great story, although I was a bit nervous about allying myself with him. I went home and thought about it and rang a prominent colleague in the business, and the result was that I got a movie deal with an international box office giant within a matter of days. I accepted an offer of IR£300,000 to write the script.

I went to my bank and revealed my imminent wealth so that they would bear with me and the constant withdrawals. I also had a couple of directing jobs on short films in the pipeline, so the future looked good. The bank more or less gave me free rein, and I was then able to write and cash cheques without a penny ever being lodged to the account. I would go into my favourite pub in the city centre day after day after day and cash cheques for £500, no problem. And that's when my using got really heavy, basically because the cash was available to me.

Very quickly, however, I reached an impasse with the subject of my story, whom I was visiting regularly in prison. He wanted me to write a sympathetic version of events, yet the more I learned about him and the gang, the more I realised that this would be next to impossible. We had a formal friendship, but he had also made vague and 'casual' threats about killing me if I didn't deliver. I was never sure how much he was 'bigging' himself up, although I knew he meant business after I met him the second time. When I came back the following week, he told me exactly where I had been, and with whom, on each of the intervening days. As he was in a maximum security prison, I was a bit rattled by this.

I was using a lot now; it was the summer of 2000. I had quite a serious habit. Using at least twice or three times daily; and that was just to function. It wasn't social. In fact I was quite mean and secretive with it. Add in a lot of alcohol, a lot of ecstasy and anything else that was going. My job lent itself to this chaotic lifestyle. I didn't have to report anywhere at 9 a.m. the next day. Sometimes, for weeks on end, I didn't have to engage with too many people. The people on a production who were in the office waiting for scripts or changes from me never passed through my mind. It was pointed out to me at least a couple of times, but I was in a 'Me Me Me' phase of life. Screw them.

I had a very wide circle of friends. Two of my friends died drugs-related deaths during this period. One beautiful girl died in horrible circumstances of a smack overdose; the other was in a car crash, caused by driving with a head full of coke. I didn't really associate either of their deaths with my drug use. I only used smack from time to time, so I wasn't bad.

I had been living on the never-never, riding the back of this film deal, thinking that when the film came out, it'd be on to Hollywood for me. This was only the beginning, so I was lending money to friends, giving it away, buying all kinds of shit. No idea. I really was quite deluded. What was needed was hard work, and it was never going to work out with that guy anyway. He was insisting that the money be split 90-10 (not the 50-50 that I suggested) because it was his life. So things quickly got out of hand there. One of his mates in the cells told him that his story was worth at least £12 million and that I was ripping him off! He's out now, just recently, and unless something happens to him I can't use this amazing story I'm sitting on.

I tried to spread my business around a few dealers. They weren't dodgy guys, by any means. In fact they were very respectable and well-to-do. But that said, I found myself in a few hairy encounters with a couple of them. I quite enjoyed that though too. I felt I was part of something illicit, which I bloody well was. I got a lot of drugs for free. Any drugs I paid for, I'd say I got at least half of that amount for free because of the people I was meeting, going to dealer parties with the big sugar bowl mounds of coke. I didn't like a lot of these dealers, but for the industry I worked in and the stories I wanted to write and talk about, it was worthwhile knowing them, worthwhile hanging out.

For a period of four years I was using daily and constantly wired. I was using other drugs as well, especially alcohol, dope and ecstasy, but cocaine was my main thing. I felt like shit a lot of the time (except directly after I'd snorted a line). Sometimes I'd get the cocaine sweats so badly that people would ask me if it was raining outside when I walked into the pub.

What happened with the bank was totally against their protocol. Neither I nor anybody in the bank signed anything. It was a gentleman's agreement of sorts that I'd be good for all this money in the near future. The sky was going to be the limit for me then and they wanted a piece of that sky. I was cashing cheques every night in a bar. I'd go in and have a couple of drinks and walk out with £500 out of the till. Sometimes they'd get pissed off with me and wouldn't do it, but rarely. I'd buy a round of drinks for the guys working in the bar and in the kitchen, just to keep them on my side. That might come to £50 and I'd write a cheque for £550. The bank called me in soon after our arrangement came into being to question why £15,000 had gone through one bar on Exchequer Street in the previous two months.

The manager asked, 'What are you spending it on?'

'Drink and drugs,' I said.

He laughed and said, 'You're an awful woman.'

I had myself in a good position with these people; I was well known and ran in the right circles.

I'd always write the last couple of cheques in the book first, so that another book would come in the post, and I ended up with a stack of cheque books. And the day it all came tumbling down was the day that I had an ounce of coke in my pocket that I had yet to pay for. The manager in the bar called me to the side—suddenly we were not so friendly any more—and told me that the last two cheques had bounced. I knew, in that instant, that the bank had shut down to me. The well had just suddenly run dry. It was a ridiculous well. I had yet to lodge anything into an account. I was spending money that wasn't mine. I think they may have written me off completely now. In fact, I more than suspect that they have.

I was having black days that I couldn't account for. Days in the week that just came and went, the duration of which I must have slept or passed out for. I knew the scam with the bank couldn't last but as long as nobody called me on it, I wasn't going to deny myself anything or worry about the outcome. And as I say, I probably have gotten away with it as regards ever reimbursing any of it. Although, I would be wary of buying a house in Ireland and being back on the radar, in case I got a knock on the door looking to repossess my stuff.

Chronologically, this account may not make much sense, but in truth it doesn't make much sense to me either. It was all a drugged haze for a period of about four years until early last year. Drug use, morning, noon and night, every day. I was the druggie film director. I was fine with that label because I was also well maintained. I dressed well and I believed I was on the up. I was certainly 'functioning' day-to-day. My apartment looked nice. My mum would turn up and I'd take her somewhere new for dinner— I'd do a couple of lines in the ladies, but I always looked the part. She knew anyway, I think, but she said nothing. My mother is a very well-preserved, clean-living professional woman. I think she felt it was part of the film scene. And it is. I've worked on documentaries about drug use, filming in the inner cities, and then gone and done those same drugs with the crew when we've finished shooting for the day.

It was potentially quite a glamorous existence, I suppose. But I was starting to make a mess of it. I'd miss my morning flight to New York to meet someone for a film and was always chasing my tail trying to catch up, always coming from the back foot and making excuses and promises to limit the damage. But then I'd get home and instead of putting my head down and doing a bit of work, I'd run out the door to a club.

In my very occasional moments of clarity I knew that I was involved in not-very-wise drug abuse and that it couldn't go on. As time passed I was beating myself up more and more about it. After a few weeks of regular blackouts I decided to go to a nice 'health spa' type place in Kerry for a fortnight's detox. I knew of it from a previous time when we had shot a feature there. It was good for me, but it wasn't a medical programme or rehab centre as such.

When I left there I moved to a friend's empty house in the back end of Carlow to get out of the scene. I ended up spending nearly five months there, effectively hiding out. Writing and fighting the urge to go out. It was a period of self-imposed isolation. It was difficult but it was my only alternative to admitting to people around me that I had a problem and going into treatment. I had caused utter chaos by having relationships with men who were unavailable to me and everything was getting ugly.

My brother was also seriously ill, but I hadn't really taken in just how ill he was. I'd call up my parents to ask if they'd seen the review of my latest short, while they were keeping a vigil at his bedside. I was utterly removed from a lot of reality. There was nothing going on for me, except *me*, until I went to Carlow. From the moment I got there, I used nothing but cannabis and alcohol. It was a great head-clearing exercise.

I'd love to go back to Dublin sometime but I don't know how warm the welcome would be from the people I abandoned. Also, two days before I left, I received a letter from the Sheriff's Office telling me they were coming to my house to take everything I owned to pay off my tax debt. I came out of my coke phase owing a shocking £100,000.

I think that a series of events coming together at one time in my life changed the way my last few years have gone. I thought I had something to celebrate with the movie deal with a US giant; I had access to all the cash I could want; and I was a big fish in an Irish puddle. I believed my own hype.

I'm living in London now. I'm part of a social scene here, where there's just as much coke and it's cheaper, but it's rubbish and I'm doing less. Last night a guy chopped out a line of coke for me that was six inches long. I thought he was trying to kill me. But it wasn't that long ago I'd have done that after my breakfast. I had better access to good coke at home. I was getting it early on in the chain, before it was stepped on by street dealers. It might have been 30 per cent pure as opposed to the 10 per cent muck that I get now. The thing about coke is that it's just so enjoyable, well, good coke is.

That said, my opinion of the drug has changed a lot. I still like the frisson of danger in my life, but I don't *have to have it.*

I don't buy the scaremongering that goes on about drugs. Of course, an A&E doctor who works at the coalface will have horror stories to tell but, apart from my two friends who died, the majority of my working and social circle are regular and 'successful' users. The incidences of sudden death are very rare.

I use now, and I enjoy it, but never ever again to the frequency that I have done in the past. I know I can control my use. I walked away from it before and I could do that again. Certain individuals close to me are trying to get me into a programme for alcohol addiction now, but that's more to do with their own fears and their own sense of what my reality should be. I know I drink a lot, and I know I have done for a long time, but I can stop—if I want to. Whenever I make a fool of myself, there's always alcohol involved, but it's part of my life and I don't have a problem with that. I don't have a single friend or colleague who doesn't drink, and drink regularly. Cutting alcohol out of my life entirely is not something I want to do or feel I need to do. Because of the nature of my work, I suppose I've never had to live a disciplined, adult life with the necessary Monday-to-Friday routine and timekeeping.

I must admit, though, that the few times in my life when I have been utterly clean and straight, I've been totally blown away by the amount I've achieved both professionally and at home. I'm the girl who lost her deal. I still have some of the traits of a rising star but I'm certainly not achieving my potential and I'm on the Revenue's hit list. But it's not too late for me to pull it all together again, you know.

I do regret talking so many great opportunities away. I got offered so many things during that period of very heavy use—potentially great projects—and I guess I blew them all. I wouldn't follow through on anything. I'd be in a bar somewhere, strung out and up since the night before, telling someone all about this deal I'd been offered, while I was missing the meeting.

I might consider a life change soon. There is a book I'd like to write, and I do get a great kick out of accomplishing really good work. I've always felt that I could do better than I have done. For the last few years I think I've been somewhat over-rated and I'd like to do something that deserves the reputation I'm trading off. But then again there's always another line, another wrap party, another free bar and sometimes they can be the most alluring things of all.

I think scientists and pharmacists should be working on a kind of a superdrug that has all of the highs and none of the lows. And legalise it. I'd use that—every day.

Chapter 9
Unlikely Friends

'For many years I've been saying that we should never underestimate the dealers. They're often dismissed as losers and pigs by the middle classes—even the ones buying from them—but that's not the case. The good ones are brilliant; they've brilliant minds for profit and cunning. They're very bright and articulate and schooled in the crafts of observation and distraction. They are brilliant. They're very skilled and it just goes to prove that if they directed their minds in another way, they'd be equally brilliant, but they've put all their focus and their skills and their development into deviousness, conning people, knocking people off.'
JOHN LONERGAN, GOVERNOR OF MOUNTJOY

——

Frank is forty-one years old and doesn't have a job. However, as the drug dealer to the employees of one of the country's leading law firms, he is kept very well, and very busy.

My customers are people with money and big offices. I deliver to the individual departments within the law firm that I supply. I have business on every floor. From the very start, my dealings have always been very civil and pleasant; nobody wants to cause a fuss by the water cooler. These are people with lives and reputations to protect. I've been dealing to the same firm for nine years now, so it's a very well-established routine for everyone concerned. It suits them and it suits me. I can operate a very profitable business without ever coming to the attention of the Gardaí.

I only deal to my regulars and I'm not looking to expand my business. I get in hash, grass, coke, heroin, speed, ecstasy—anything they want. Over the last five years or so, the coke business has rocketed—that's what most of my buyers want. I like to make about 250 per cent profit on the coke I buy in. I make a trip into town twice a week and deliver to their desks and to their cars. I never do any business in pubs or clubs. Most of my customers are very discreet family men and women. If they want to meet with me over the weekend for any more, then I will come to their houses. That's my rule. I'm very courteous in my transactions, as are they. If there's any messing, then I don't do business with them again.

———

Gordon is well established in the criminal underworld in Dublin. Previously he supplemented his income with drug dealing around the IFSC, but he retired from this because he was starting to attract too much police attention. He operated efficiently through a policy of fear, which he is proud to recall.

People were afraid of me. They had to be. I mainly dealt coke to the suits down at the docks, but because they weren't criminals, they mightn't be aware of my reputation. They might think they were better than me and that I didn't need paying on time. But they'd soon learn. I did my dealing out of my car. I'd deliver. I didn't want them coming to my house at all hours. I've other businesses to protect. If I was owed money I'd send someone to visit them at work, in their fancy office. I'd make an example of one of them every so often. If I had to, I'd stand on one of their fucking heads in the car park so they wouldn't forget who the boss was in our arrangement.

———

Governor of Mountjoy Prison, John Lonergan says that he often hears middle-class people up in arms demanding to know who's supplying their children with drugs: 'It's actually his next-door neighbour, it's his school pal, it's the fellow sitting beside him in Blackrock College or in Gonzaga or whatever. He's not coming down from Mars or driving in from Ballymun.

'There are a lot of kids going to secondary school making a nice little income out of it. They're buying tablets and they're buying cannabis and they're buying cocaine; mainly I suppose ecstasy and cannabis and they're selling it out, making €4 or €5 a go. A few of those deals would quickly mount up for a kid. You could work in Centra all weekend or you could be the popular lad or girl at school this way. I always tell parents not to be looking away for these fellas coming in with the drugs as if they were driving around the neighbourhood in a big car with tinted windows. They should just look to their own.

'A cleaner here in the prison, a fantastic inner-city Dublin woman, was telling me that she saved very hard to send her two boys out to the southside to get them out of the city drug culture. So out to a private secondary school with them. And her eldest comes home after the first week and tells her, 'They're all dealing, Mum. They're all dealing drugs out there. More than I've ever seen.'

——

Maisie is nearly twenty-nine years old. A very striking blonde woman, when we meet in the Westbury Hotel she causes heads to turn. She studied maths at college and has a PhD. She's an accountant now, but previously enjoyed a career as a drug dealer.

As a thirteen-year-old child, Maisie attended an Irish-speaking school in Dublin. She spent a lot of time cycling her lilac *Bianca* bike—the one she'd had since the Christmas two years before—around the neighbourhood.

If she had a bit of business to attend to, she'd cycle into a flat complex in the south inner city and back to Milltown. If she pedalled fast, it would only take about twenty-five minutes to get there. Assuming she didn't have too long to wait and there was a guy around to do business with her, she'd be back home within the hour. She'd usually do the cycle home with her swag in fifteen minutes. She puts her increased speed down to the rush of adrenaline, fear, panic and excitement. At this early stage of her career, the plaid bag on the back of her bike would typically contain as much marijuana as £50—stolen from her dad's wallet—would get her. She'd sell it to her school friends for twice that.

The first time I ever tried any drugs was when I was at the Gaeltacht on a day trip to Inishmore. I was twelve and was hanging around with some boys. One of them had a supply of hash. It was thrilling, hiding behind the rocks smoking joints and speaking English. My memory of that first day is of the sense of adventure, the freedom and the romance of it all.

In the months previous, kids around me had taken to inhaling Tipp-Ex thinners but I wasn't interested in that. But this, this was my thing. When I came back from the Gaeltacht I took it upon myself to find out where I could get some of this hash. I found out about guys in Ballyfermot who were selling it. I'd never been to Ballyfermot. I didn't know where it was. It amazes me now—when I recall it—that I had the motivation and the wherewithal to find it and get myself there at that age. Initially, I'd buy enough for myself and two of my friends and we'd share it out in my bedroom when I got home. Three twelve-year-old girls with braces on our teeth smoking dope in the afternoons.

I copped on early enough that as I was the one making the effort to go and to buy the stuff, then I should buy as much as I could with money I'd taken from my dad's wallet and sell it on to them at a profit. I also started smoking it by myself, before I met them, after my homework in the evenings, and before I went to bed.

Once I was shown where to get it, I went through a phenomenal phase. My 'progression' happened really quickly; there was this immense drive within me. I applied myself to drug taking and selling like I'd never applied myself to anything before. I changed dealer and started heading into the flats in town. I was a child and yet I had this astonishing commitment to buying, selling and using drugs and the entire cloak-and-dagger goings on that came with it.

By the time I was fifteen, I was smoking dope every day—before school, during school, on the way home, in the evenings before camogie practice, out the back window of my house late at night. I was also now using ecstasy and acid several nights a week. The 'magic drawer' in my bedroom was never empty. I was earning a tidy sum and had developed a reputation in the school. I'd be inundated with orders before parties or discos. I dealt to the whole school at this stage, from the eleven-year-olds to the eighteen-year-olds. Business boomed.

Nobody noticed at home—or if they did, they didn't say. They probably put my distance and lack of any real engagement with them down to typical pubescent behaviour. The first time it dawned on me that I might not be as in control of it all as I would have liked was around the time of my Inter Cert mocks. I remember thinking I should try stopping for a few weeks and get my head down to study. That was the first time I'd tried to exert any control over my own habit, and I couldn't. Not for a day. I was taken aback. I knew nothing about 'addiction'—I was a child. What did I know about such a grown-up thing?

Over the years I had found different places and made different connections. I'd conduct a fair bit of business sitting on the toilet under the stairs at home with the cream phone from the hall table on my lap. At the grand old age of sixteen, I was standing outside flats and sitting in pokey living rooms that smelt of stew, counting my pound notes across a table. I had a new bike now, an impressive red, ten-speed racer that I got for Christmas, but it had no bag attached so I'd have to take a rucksack with me on my back. The company I kept was just shocking—the people I knew, the people who knew me, my name, my home phone number.

I remember clearly a school trip in fifth year, back to the bloody Aran Islands again. I recall feeling under pressure. It was a massive operation for me to orchestrate getting the drugs for everyone in time, dealing them out to the others on the journey there, rolling loads of joints, worrying that one of the less discreet kids would get caught and dob me in, teachers looming at every turn.

I particularly liked a smoke before studying, although this urge occasionally was a pain in the ass, more like a burden. My mind was preoccupied with maintaining this habit and sometimes, for a minute, I just wanted the freedom to focus on my exams. Drugs definitely dominated my thoughts. I had no interest in boys or any normal things. My mind was filled with using and buying drugs—when and where will I get it, what will I do with it, how much will I sell, how much will I keep, how much will I make.

After I managed to complete my Leaving Cert, I went to college in Galway and lived in a house with a couple of friends who had a similar relationship with drugs as I did. Within six weeks, I had a network of buyers in Galway. I had cut my teeth at home in Dublin but now it was the big time. I had more freedom and I realised the potential of the whole thing—the scale of the demand and the money to be made. Far smarter than getting some waitressing job like the other girls. Also, my father's pocket wasn't around to back me up so I needed to up the ante to survive. In short, I started dealing out of the house in quite a visible way. I had suppliers in Dublin and in Galway and I was making a ridiculous amount of money for an eighteen- or nineteen-year old. Maybe £900 or £1,000—that's pounds, a decade ago!—each week in profit. I started shafting people and I never shared my own stuff anymore. I had friends who had been in my life since I was very small but if they didn't have the cash, then I'd nothing for them.

I got incredibly mean and hung up on profits and deals. I was a businesswoman now. The enterprise that I could have had going if I hadn't been using the stuff myself! I hadn't the brains to keep my own head clear. I didn't worry about what I was doing. The only anxiety I felt was when I'd be meeting a supplier and it could be somewhere really dodgy. I was really lucky because in all of the years I was only ripped off by guys selling to me on two occasions—and I was never hurt personally. I had no comprehension of the fear that I should have felt alone with money in these dark places. I walked around with a head full of acid. God knows what could have happened.

Halfway through my third year I got busted by the cops. I was on my way out to a nightclub one night when I got picked up by the Gardaí. They put me into a van and then in a cell overnight. The officers strip-searched me and found hash and E. It was pretty horrible as I had my period at the time and they weren't being nice at all. They charged me the next morning. Three charges: possession and intent on hash, and possession of E. They had a warrant and went back to the house. They found a lot more in the house and also about £2,000, which they took. When they told me about the money, that was what broke me. Then the tears came. Isn't that odd? I actually felt bereft without my money. I loved money. Money had always been a big thing for me. My sense of having to have my own money started before the drugs, and removing that from me meant I'd have to ask my dad for money.

I was released and my court date was set for some months later. Because of the court case, the story was in the papers, names were mentioned, and articles were written that made it look like I was sitting in the canteen selling heroin from a stall. Middle-class Milltown knew all about me now! Suddenly my family noticed me and made noises about the signs being there, and old school friends—most of them former paying customers of mine—were full of stories about my dealing in the corridors. It was hard for my parents.

I was worried about what would happen to me if I was convicted. I wanted to have a career and a nice quality of life. I made a swift about-turn and started to apply myself to college like never before. Over the next few weeks, I stopped dealing and then I stopped using. I started going to college every day, having not been for more than a month in total over the previous year and a half.

Now I was there—at the front, with a pencil. I was like: 'Feed me! I need to excel and to get out of here and make money. Quick! Before I change my mind'. I became quite obsessive. I had to be the best. Miss Dropout became Miss First Class Honours. Always extremes. Never steady.

When the court date came around, I got the Probation Act which means that I actually don't have a record. I haven't touched any drugs since, but I'm still not comfortable being around them. About two years ago, I picked up a box of matches at a party and there was a lump of dope in it. I just froze. I couldn't deal with it at all. I had to leave. I've come a long way and I can't look back. I'm an accountant now, but I still don't make as much money as I did when I was a kid in digs.

———

'About a decade ago, I was a computer gimp who did drugs on the side. Soon afterwards, I realised I could make a living out of taking my hobby mainstream. I've been a drugs gimp who does computers on the side ever since. But I'm probably the most law-abiding citizen in the hood. If I went around to the local cop shop and asked them to sign my picture for a passport, they wouldn't recognise me. They've never met me, they don't know me, I've no criminal record. I don't need to draw any attention to myself whatso-ever. I know there are at least two other drug dealers on this beautiful Victorian square but I don't know who they are or where they are; I've no interest.

I'm not an 'evil drug dealer'. I'm quite a moral and ethical person who happens to bang out some drugs rather than a nefarious ne'er-do-well. I'm not selling crack in schools, you know. Compared to the pills that are being prescribed by your average doctor, I'm a bloody saint. I'm never going to feed anyone Prozac or Xanax or tell them to take three Valium every day. People are eating Xanax, Prozac, Valium. These might take the sting away at the time but the after-effects are absolutely lethal.'

Ryan has been dealing drugs around Dublin for almost ten years. He previously dealt in all drugs, but he has recently scaled back and dropped the very busy cocaine business because it had become 'too messy'. Now he supplies hash, grass and ecstasy.

Business is steady and solid—he's not interested in expanding; too much exposure, too much grief.

'Of course, if the taxman came knocking, I'd have some explaining to do. Living here with no discernible income and declaring nothing: "This man exists in limbo, no money coming in and not a lot going out." But it's not like there's a fleet of candy-coloured sports cars in my garage.'

He's not joking. In fact, Ryan lives in the grottiest basement flat that I have ever stepped into. He apologises that it is a mess 'from the mad parade through it over the St Patrick's weekend', but the dust is at least a year old. The window sills are piled high with bits of rubbish and a broken vase. He has cleared a couple of 'flat surfaces' so we can sit and talk. This tiny room is three sides couches—one more hideously misshapen and stained than the other. The only other things in the room are several large towering cream-coloured PCs and a number of black add-ons that look like bomb timers from *The A-Team*. Cables run across much of the crawling carpet. While I'm there, a guy arrives in through the still open front door and—without a word—looks up cheap flights on one of the computers.

Recently I've hardened against cocaine because I've seen it just mess people's heads up so many times. It did it to me. Coke turns you into an arsehole. I mean anyone who takes it will have to concede the point. Most people who do cocaine for a long period of time—where are they? Up in a back bedroom somewhere with a load of ex-models snorting lines, and talking about coke, and where to get good coke, and how quickly they can get coke. It gets pretty fucking lame after a few years and their conversations tend to become rather dull. You're not going to get too many people so strung out for a lump of hash at three o'clock in the morning that they have to come round and knock on your window. But heroin users or cokeheads you will; you'll get them arriving in at all hours—a convoy of three cars; ding, ding, ding, ding—you got any blow?! That sort of madness happens all the time with coke and the customers are just too volatile. There are a lot of lunatics involved in it and there's big money in it. But the risks are equally big. When someone asks for coke now I say I don't move in those circles anymore.

It's coming down in price and coming down in quality. I mean any of the cocaine I've seen in the last year or so has been rubbish. Once you adulterate coke and chop it down three or four times it's rubbish. Most people who are using it get some white powder and a piece of paper and they throw it into their heads and they've already had six pints or whatever, so it's a placebo effect a lot of the time. Generally you have to have a job if you're doing coke, and then you generally end up without one after the whole experience. It's a messy path to be on.

My customers are everybody from concert violinists through to solicitors and journalists. I keep away from the head-the-balls. Most of my regulars are soft, Southside, middle-class types like myself. They call into me here, they sit down, have a cup of tea or whatever. They're here for a short while and then they head off with their gear. There isn't a queue of people out the door with suitcases of money or anything glamorous like that.

I changed supplier last year. The guy I get my gear from now is a Nigerian businessman. He's quiet like me. He doesn't want to rock the boat, doesn't need the cops following him around and that's fine with me. I'm in exactly the same position. I've no interest in having the cops hassling me, so he can trust me to be quiet and I can trust him to be the same. He's going six or seven days a week—flat out with the business. I meet him in town so he doesn't know where I live. I don't know where he lives. We don't chat. He doesn't tell me anything. I don't tell him anything.

Occasionally you get droughts in supply. For whatever reason you'll get a drought that might last for a couple of weeks and then dealers tend to root out the old dried-up rubbish that they had lying around and bang that out, but it's the only stuff that's available the odd time. That'll happen every year coming up to Christmas, for instance. From late November there's often a drought and suddenly all this rubbish comes on the market at twice the price, but sure that's just business. This guy has two or three different sources so it's rare that I'd have a problem.

There are a number of suppliers who'll bang you out nine-bars—which is 250 grams of hash—and you can get them as easily as you get bread and milk. It's not in their interest to be selling things by the ounce or by the quarter or whatever. That's just too much trouble. So I go to one of these guys and get four bars and then call back to him in a week or two. I'm very unlikely to be busted because my pattern hasn't changed over the last nine or ten years. For anyone who's moved in to houses around me, this was the way things always were so there's nothing unusual or new going on that will draw attention to me. I've been lucky. I don't fool myself that I'm totally safe or anything like that though. Complacency isn't part of the game. I live an exceedingly quiet life.

Dublin has been pretty much dry of decent pills for the last six months which is extremely unusual. You get all kinds of weird pill-shaped things that certainly are not MDMA. You can put anything in a pill. As long as it makes you feel a bit odd, you'll think you're high. That is the big problem. At least with a lump of hash—you have the hash, you can burn it, you can smell it, you can see it is good stuff, you can smoke a joint of it and you know where you stand. With the powders and the pills, it could be anything. I mean I could be giving you horse tranquillisers or anything that makes you feel a bit strange. I can say, 'Well, that's an effect, that's the effect of the pill,' but you could be swallowing industrial chemicals, any-thing. Lots of the pills I see, I wouldn't touch. Pure dangerous. People take them and have some bizarre and very dangerous reactions. That's the main crime that goes on. Because they're illegal, people can poison you and there's no comeback. You can't exactly wander down to the cop shop saying, 'I can't feel my left side because I took a pill off this guy last night,' because they'll book you for buying pills.

Drug users should be made aware of the unfortunate fact that when you take your drugs, just as you're going to go up, you have to acknowledge that afterwards you're going to come back down. People who don't accept that and who take drugs to bring themselves back up when they feel down, that's a fool's game. Just like alcoholics, they'll wake up and they'll have the Hair of the Dog to cure them, as opposed to keeping away from booze for two or three days after being on a binge.

With E, there's a serious comedown. What goes up must come down and it's a serotonin imbalance in your brain. It's a physical thing. It's not just 'I feel a bit groggy today.' When you take a load of pills at the weekend, you'll be sitting there on a damp Tuesday morning thinking it's all a bleak, empty existence. If you can register in your brain how this isn't real, things aren't that bleak, it's just a lack of serotonin, you can get through it. If you don't take that into account you might just end up hanging from the rafters, and a lot of people do.

Other dealers that I know push heroin to take the edge off your comedown. This was a very common practice when E went through its major popularity in Ireland. A lot of people took a tonne of E, and the following day would be feeling jittery and 'Sure here, chase the dragon, or whatever, have a bit of heroin, just a small bit to take the edge off and you'll feel grand.' And then, of course, a lot of those people stopped doing the E in the first place and just concentrated on the heroin. And then they did more and more heroin, and then they were dead. You didn't see them in the nightclub anymore. They were just gone.

Likewise, if someone's doing a lot of coke, the following day they're going to be a bit gritty, a bit edgy. Doing a little heroin will bring them down all right, but if they're stupid enough to try heroin these days then I've got no time for them. There's plenty of education, there's plenty of stuff on record, there's plenty of bad, bad stories about heroin misuse. It's not an unknown quantity, it's not something that's being hidden, kids are taught about it in school. If you go out and try heroin, fuck you, that's just stupidity at this stage. It's like crack cocaine; you see enough shots of people with no teeth, and their lives totally destroyed.

You can seem to be reasonably lucid on coke, *if* you're dealing with people who don't know about coke. But if your boss used to do a bit of coke, he'll spot you. I can tell cokeheads from a mile off. They're very emphatic and focused but if you actually listen to what they're saying it's the same bullshit, just faster and again and again and again. Coke's great for a while but then you get your lifetime's quota and it becomes a little tedious. Hopefully you can survive it that long without destroying everything you've got.

The downside of hash, especially for people who are smoking grass, is that occasionally you do get bouts of paranoia and you can get psychosis. I've seen it happen, but a lot of these people were going that way anyway. The hash might push you over the edge, if you're leaning that way already. By the same token, if you're feeling a bit twitchy then maybe drinking a half bottle of whiskey isn't going to improve your disposition.

If you smoke hash or grass for weeks continuously, it will have an effect just as if you go to the pub every day as soon as it opens and drink until closing. Excess is always excess, but with hash you've to go pretty far to get excessive. With cocaine or whiskey you don't have to go that far at all. If you sit there and snort your way through an eight-ball of coke, something bad might well happen to you. Likewise, if you sit there and drink two bottles of whiskey, you might just cause some trouble. If you have a couple of joints of grass, you're going to slump off to the shops, buy some chocolate and go home for a snooze.

Most people who smoke hash are reasonable, civilised, middle-class types. They're not going to rock the boat. They'd love legalised hash but they're not going to sign any petitions or anything like that. They'll leave that to the students.

Political correctness means anyone can say anything they like against drugs but nobody can say a word in their defence. A kid might smoke a joint at a party, maybe get sick after, and then smoke another one. He'll quickly realise that he hasn't grown any horns or died, as he'd been warned. And that's the danger of this excessive political correctness. The kid might decide to be hung for a sheep as a lamb, you know. Having tried hash and not experienced a major psychotic episode as he'd been assured by his parents or whoever, it's reasonable that a kid might think the same must be true of what's been said about the dangers of coke and heroin. He can go and try coke and heroin and maybe you'll find him floating down the canal some months later.

I see nothing wrong with what I'm doing and I've no plans to stop. My family and some friends know nothing whatsoever about my business. They think I'm just working from home on my computer gimpy thing.

Technically what I'm doing is illegal, but the way I look at it is if you were selling a bit of whiskey during prohibition in America, were you an evil person, or was there a stupid law around saying you couldn't buy booze and you were just subverting it?

Chapter 10
Treatment

'NA *meetings and treatment centres are like restau-*
rants. Different ones in different areas come in and
out of fashion at different times, in different seasons,
and depending on who's in the kitchen. What was
good last year might not be in vogue now; a different
crowd, a different scene.'
ALAN, COMPOSER

The Rutland Centre is a residential centre in Templeogue, South
Dublin, specialising in the treatment of alcohol, drug and gam-
bling dependencies as well as eating disorders. The ratio of men
to women in the residential unit is three to two. Stephen Rowen
is Clinical Director.

One of the risks we have here when clients leave treatment is someone putting drugs under their noses within a day of their leaving. A
good dealer will be in touch within twenty-four hours. When people
go into detox at Beaumont Hospital, it's a locked unit and the reason
for that is not to keep people in—people can sign themselves out
any time they want—it's to keep people out, to keep out the dealers.

There are no mobile phones here. This is a kind of a sanctuary. A zero-tolerance, total abstinence-based, drug-free treatment programme. There is no methadone here, there's no benzodiazepine, there are no anti-depressants, there are no illegal street drugs, there's no Nurofen Plus—nothing. The idea is that you feel your feelings and, as sad or as difficult as that might be, we will give you and the other clients will give you tremendous therapeutic support. There's no medication.

It's very closed. We don't want our clients going across the road, stopping by the Off Licence, or making a phone call to their dealer, so movement is very restricted. More people will tell you they hate to leave than will tell you they hate to stay. The world out there hasn't changed. There's temptation on every corner as soon as they leave.

Pain is the first gift of recovery. It's not that I'm sadistic and want everybody to be in pain but it's pain that brings you in the door. I think people don't stop abusing drugs if their bank account is pretty healthy and they're having fun and they're partying, and nobody's mad at them and they're not having any hassles at work, and there's no interference from the courts or the police. Those people aren't looking for help. The ones looking for help are in pain. Perhaps their partner has given them an ultimatum or they've just burned out the bank account.

The one thing all our clients have in common is addiction, and all people with addiction have a progressive condition. There's a certain amount of denial, a certain amount of leaning on others, a certain amount of irresponsibility, and a huge amount of self-centredness and self-pity. There's also an interesting hierarchy that always emerges; the cocaine addicts look down on the heroin addicts and the alcoholics look down on the drug addicts and the gamblers look down on everybody.

Yesterday we brought in three new clients, so we have twenty-four clients in treatment at the moment. Those three people filled the slots of three people who left the previous day. We try to mix young and old, men and women, drugs and alcohol, people who would be very well off with people much less so and then everybody else in between. I've worked in or visited nearly thirty treatment centres in my career and I think the Rutland has the best mix. So many programmes are elitist and only for the well off, the upper middle class, and then others solely for the great unwashed, for the publicly funded clients.

I'm very passionate about the extra added advantage of the mixed social economic grouping. I think it makes the sense of community stronger and the experience deeper and broader. That said, I've no doubt that programmes exclusively for the more middle and upper classes of people are doing some good work. If you have a caring professional who sits with a client who's in trouble with a chemical and looks them in the eye and asks the right questions, asks the tough questions, offers some kind of hope, encouragement and support, well then some people can become miracle stories.

————

Drug users who wish to avail of the services of the Drug Treatment Centre Board can walk in off the street and be provided with a rapid assessment of their needs. Set up in 1969, it is the longest established treatment service in Ireland. Originally located in Jervis Street Hospital, it is now located on Pearse Street. Out-patient treatment facilities are provided on-site. In-patient detoxification facilities are located in Beaumont and Cherry Orchard Hospitals. A National Drug Analysis Laboratory service provides screening and toxicology tests. These screening tests show an increase in drug use—cocaine in particular—countrywide and in every social class.

However, for the majority of middle-class users interviewed, treatment within the publicly supported treatment system was something they dismissed outright. The typical user who wished to avail of help would only consider treatment in a private, secluded setting and among individuals of a similar socio-economic status.

'Any idiot can get someone off drugs in four or five weeks—I can get someone off drugs in a matter of weeks—but I can't keep them off them. I'm not there on a rainy Tuesday evening when they've had a bad day and they're looking out the window and there's nothing to do. How can I stop them then? That's where Narcotics Anonymous comes in. That's when they leave the house and go to a meeting and it maintains them to get through until the next day,' says Dr Tom Lacey.

'When a person comes through the door looking for help with a drug habit, I usually send them to NA for a period of three months. If they can't make it by themselves there, then I would recommend they attend the Rutland Centre for a six-week period. All the studies show that residential care gets the best results in the long term. Out-patients and methadone? In my opinion, they're a waste of time.

'You need to get into an addict's head, dismantle it, and put it back together again. Twenty-four hours a day is necessary for that. If they can't make it through NA and Rutland, then I'm not interested. Why should I care more about somebody than they care about themselves? I can carry the message, but I can't carry the person.

'Narcotics Anonymous attacks the disease of isolation at its root because the power of the group and the meeting removes the feeling of being alone. The fellowships are a safe and anonymous place for people to go where everyone is as good as everyone else, where there is absolute equality, respect and democracy among all. It provides an atmosphere where you can share your innermost feelings and all of your fears. It's quite revelatory to attend meetings and to hear men and women talk about their darkest fears. It is a safe cradle for them; the group holds all this shit and

then the person can walk out and leave it there and it will never be
mentioned again.'

———

**Located just outside the picturesque village of Laragh in County
Wicklow, 'Forest' is the residential treatment centre with the
highest fees. Only in its third year, this luxurious 'guest house'
seems to have already found its niche market, catering largely for
middle-aged, affluent women with substance abuse difficulties.**

**Forest accommodates eight clients at a time in private rooms,
with all meals cooked by the in-house gourmet chef and nutri-
tionist. Based on principles of trust and motivation, residential
care is offered in three- and four-week periods. With its trusting
and non-confrontational approach, Forest provides a different—
and in this country—unique methodology for tackling drug
addiction. The Sick Doctors Scheme has approved it for its
members. Specialising in addiction, Colin O'Driscoll is a Senior
Psychologist at Forest.**

Therapy goes on three days per week, Monday, Wednesday and
Friday, and everything outside of that is about treating the whole
person and being comfortable in the environment. In the morning, guests have a one-to-one session with a psychologist and in
the afternoon they have a group therapy session, which is run by
one of the counsellors. The rest of the time is taken up with different creative activities—art, yoga, massage and long walks. Walks
are something that we really try to integrate as much as possible.
The surroundings are so beautiful and walking is physical, confi-
dence-building, and highly beneficial for clearing the cobwebs.

This is not a locked centre. Guests can come and go freely. Giving
individuals the responsibility to make their own decisions makes

them autonomous throughout their stay. This means that we don't get the catapulting effect when people leave and are suddenly faced with all their decisions again. We find that the trust system works. We find that when you give people the ability to choose they often make the right choice for themselves. If people relapse, they will be asked to leave, but it's not a blanket policy. It's written in our literature that they can be asked to leave. It often happens that people slip up, recognise the fact, and want to pull through. They might get through their slip and feel more confident as a result, and maybe they will have identified a new trigger that they hadn't seen before. Therapeutically, we can work with that. It does happen and people re-state their commitment and come back into the programme.

We have aftercare in the form of one-to-one sessions and group therapies in our office on Fitzwilliam Street in Dublin. Unfortunately, the nature of our work means that we see the same faces here time and again.

We have a very high women to men ratio, about 8 to 1. Perhaps this is because women find it more appropriate to come to a place like this—a very private set-up. But often referrals are through GPs, counsellors and psychologists. The age group is predominantly between forty and sixty years. Our clients are professional career people who can make decisions about what best suits them. That said, it wouldn't be entirely unusual to have a twenty-year-old guy who has been smoking heroin for the past two years sitting beside a middle-aged accountant who is very established in her career and abusing prescription tablets. We treat everything from codeine-based addictions to heroin. The most common would be painkillers and cocaine. The only people we will not accept are users who inject. This is part of our commitment to the local community. We also don't detox people and it's quite obvious to see somebody in a detoxing period. If they are still in that detoxing period, we won't accept them. They are welcome to come back when they are clean.

The average person has probably been in at least one treatment centre before coming to us, so we tend not to be the first port of call. I think Forest works, and I think that the privacy is a big draw. If it was me, I would want to be assured of some sort of exclusivity or at least that my confidentiality was protected; I wouldn't want to be paraded down a main street.

At Forest we treat the person. We don't place emphasis on the family or loved ones. It is part of the responsibility of clients to give you their full story. They can lead us up the garden path if they want to, and in some ways they might succeed, but most often they don't. We're not going to go to somebody else to get the information. I find that wherever a client is taking me in a therapy session, it tends to be an important place to go. If it's a diversion, there's something within that diversion that is important too. We don't test clients for drugs. It's all trust based.

If we bring somebody in and sit on them for six weeks and lock the doors around them, they are unlikely to change in any real and voluntary way. What we do is empower people to be autonomous and have decision-making abilities, to develop the confidence and have the courage to make decisions about their own behaviour. What we do is based on respect. I believe in the approach here. We don't employ the punitive element to addiction and treatment that you see throughout Ireland and the UK.

———

'I've worked in a number of places and I can safely say this: Nowhere has got the answer. No place has got all the answers and there are faults in every single treatment system.'
COUNSELLOR ROLANDE ANDERSON

I worked for twenty years in St Patrick's Hospital and I loved it. Adored it. But you think you know a lot, and really, you know nothing. Someone new will always walk through the door and challenge everything you think you've learned about the human condition. I was the Senior Social Worker and Assistant Director in St Pat's. For eighteen years I also ran the spouses group for the partners of addicts.

I am pro-Narcotics Anonymous. I'm pro anything that helps. Absolutely. There's not a lot we can offer, you see. In terms of offering people sustained help, there's not a lot on offer out there. The most important thing is self-help and to meet other people who have been through the same. If I can put a new client—full of terror and shame—in touch with someone whom I know to be decent, reliable and willing to help, who has also been through the same ordeal of addiction that they are now experiencing, and who is happy to give their time and to talk to them, then I will. It's a great way to begin chipping away at a lot of the fear and the secrecy and horror that they're carrying.

Another positive thing is that most people who are in recovery themselves have no agenda. They will help because they want to. It's as simple as that. If the person ends up going along to an NA meeting and finding support there, then that's great. It's twenty-four hours, whereas professional staff are restricted to certain hours and time slots and may not be available when needed. In the early days, I do think that the level of support offered by NA can be very important. And it's experience that has led me to believe this.

Sometimes there can be one isolated moment—a tipping moment—that can tip a person into either profound depression and suicidal tendencies, or into recovery. Some people do suddenly decide to change when they have that tipping moment, when they hit the point that I call their 'personal skid row'. It used to be the case that people would talk about a person having to reach 'rock bottom' before they could change. The problem with rock bottom is that it may be death, or living on the streets. A personal skid row is the depth to which a person is willing to go—be it spiritually or emotionally or whatever—before they realise that their life is on the verge of collapse and they cannot let this continue. For example, yesterday one of my new clients who has presented herself for treatment said that when she saw the look on her child's face, she realised that she had to stop.

Another client of mine who went to an NA meeting this morning told me afterwards that he felt totally isolated when he was there, because he had nothing like the horror stories that he was hearing around him. And yet he has terrible problems with his own dignity, with maintaining relationships, and with family ties. They are his horrors, and are just as valid. It is important, in a group, that people identify but don't compare.

I think class can be an issue with treatment. But people do tend to find their own meeting. They tend to gravitate toward a meeting that suits them and their needs. But there's no accounting for that. The joke is that if you live in Dalkey, you go to the meeting in Sutton and if you live in Sutton, you go to the Dalkey meetings. So you've an equal chance of meeting someone you know. And yet, sometimes I've sent very 'respectable' clients to a meeting that I thought might suit them and they've hated it; hated the snobbery, the cliquey element. Instead they've found their feet in the inner city, in places that are as rough as they come, and they've loved it; loved the honesty, loved that it's real. This is certainly not the norm, but there's often no accounting for what works.

Forest is exclusive, it's very expensive and it's new. I'd be happy to give it the benefit of the doubt. It's trying something new. They have a different approach completely to the Twelve-Step Programme. It's based on motivational interviewing, and in my opinion there's a limit to what that can do with addiction. There's a naïvety in it really. I'm all for self-determination and respecting people and autonomy, but you could argue that someone who is heavily addicted—by definition—hasn't got autonomy and simply isn't in a position to take control of themselves at that time.

This business is always trial and error, and not all therapies will suit everyone. I have a very open mind about different therapies but occasionally I do come across something that I know is just not going to work and I'll say it.

No mainstream centre will take a person with an addiction problem until they are clean. They will not be entertained, which is a funny paradox, isn't it? Where do you go then? In an ideal world, you would have a central referral agency that would bring you in for an assessment, and where someone can say, 'I really want to stop, but I can't. I need help stopping.' And they would send you, in the first instance, to a detox centre before seeing you again for the next step. Or go to such and such a place—be it Forest, St John of God's, the Rutland, St Patrick's Hospital, the USA, or see a person individually, or whatever is felt would best suit your individual needs. Ideally, this kind of an independent assessment with no vested financial interests or otherwise is what I'd love to see. Just a genuine interest in each person. The public services, in terms of treatment, are just appalling. Appalling. It is scary how little there is at a public level for someone addicted to drugs.

I've been doing assessments for over twenty years—I still do assessments—and I've seen all kinds of things. I see people every week who are not ready for counselling and who need to do a treatment centre; people who have been messed up by treatment centres; people who have been totally screwed over by different approaches. Traditionally, some dreadful things went on in terms of bullying and confrontational approaches in different places. People would have been beaten up here in the past for having an addiction problem; certainly beaten up emotionally, if not also physically. Somewhere in the middle is probably the best approach.

An old colleague of mine used to say that to be a therapist you have to be an idealist without delusions. I think that's nice. You have to have an awareness of the nature of addiction, and at the same time respect the individual and value the individual's rights. It can be tricky; it's a fine line to walk.

——

'Drugs are a real fixation. You become that great character in The Hobbit, *Gollum: "My precious, my precious." He is such a great metaphor for what addiction is, the young being that becomes a weird, strange, obsessed and horrid creature that will do anything to get the ring.'*

Last year, Kieran spent $1,000 a day on treatment, 'eating horrible cafeteria food' for three weeks in the exclusive Cottonwood Treatment Centre in Arizona. A thirty-nine-year-old millionaire, he is a beneficiary of the dot.com revolution. In 1998 he founded an online gambling company and simultaneously acquired a very expensive drug habit.

I could have any drugs that I fancy here, on this table in this five-star hotel, in the next half hour. Even though I'm not in the loop anymore. I'd make a call and go outside. Within fifteen minutes or so, I'd get into the dealer's car and drive around the block. He would slide my order between the seats. That seems to be a universal move. Anywhere in the world I've been and bought drugs they've been slid back to me between the seats. More often than not, there'd be some bored-looking girl in the seat next to me. In New York, my dealer drove an amazing Lincoln with a DVD player and had three or four phones going all the time. You know when your dealer drives a better car than you and is telling you about his recent five-star trip around Japan that there's something not quite right.

I went through college as a bit of a stoner. I was very much the 'what's up dude' guy. I did a six-week road trip across America and spent time at Rocky Mountain Nashville Park—that kind of dippy behaviour. But then, at thirty, I moved to New York City and became a cliché. All of a sudden I would only wear Gucci shirts and all of that. I would go out to restaurants every night and spend a fortune on food that I never ate, because I'd be in the toilet snorting lines of coke and my appetite would vanish. It was all hideously expensive and when I'm driving around the country here now, I think about the properties I could buy outright if I could get a refund on that lifestyle.

I lived for four years in New York and I've been living between Dublin and London for the last five. When I was in New York it was the latter end of the dot.com madness. Everyone felt like a master of the universe, you know, and greed and money took over. It's amazing how much you can really upset values. I went from teaching in a high school for four years and coaching tennis at the weekends to moving to New York and starting a dot.com company. All of a sudden, I was thinking, 'I could become a millionaire, a multi-millionaire, overnight.' And I was right.

I had an idea to start a gaming company, an online gambling business, with another guy. We got it going and owned it fifty/fifty. Within a year, we had raised $9 million and built up a team of sixty people. We had the exclusive contracts to various sporting events. I was hyped up on adrenaline and stress and we were bringing in an awful lot of money.

I had a Masters in the Humanities. What did I know about cash flow, supporting sixty people and all of that? But it seemed like I blinked, and all of a sudden there we were, making money. My partner was no better qualified than I was. We were just winging it and flying by the seat of our pants. Hardly the time to start doing coke—when you're running your own start-up business—but I did. I hadn't ever touched it until I got to New York and then it was just as common as candy, literally, little packs all over the place right in full view. I wouldn't ask if you were offended or bothered; I'd just snort it wherever. Now that I think about it, I can see how even though they might have been smiling and being fine, there were many people who were disgusted by it . . . by me.

I was on one track, and it went very quickly from the odd night out to every single time I had a drink, which was about four nights a week. In the early stages, I'd use with a group of guys. Someone would beep a dealer and the next thing you know it'd be 3 a.m. and you're playing pool and trying to track down the dealer again. God forbid that he'd actually respond at that stage, because it would mean you'd be going straight into work from the poolroom the next day.

The drugs weren't enhancing my performance at work. I had enormous reserves of stamina and energy, but to this day I don't know how I ever pulled it off, quite frankly. But the more you do pull it off, the more you think, 'I can do anything. There's no keeping me down.'

Those first couple of hours at my desk when I'd either not slept at all or I'd have slept on a couch for an hour, would be hellish. I'd look like shit, slugging away at three, four and five large espressos, one after another, waiting for the adrenaline to take over. But then, in the slog of the dot.com businesses, everyone is looking like shit and like they've had too much coffee. So I might not have stood out too much . . .?

I'd be either so burnt out that next evening that I couldn't even think about it, or I'd hear myself saying, 'We'll just go to happy hour and have a cocktail.' I'd usually be doing three nights in a row with no sleep. I was the primary mover in my business but still I would have to call in sick and make up lies. My business partner was a very healthy, rock-climbing sort and he didn't tolerate drugs. I very quickly got to the point where I started hiding it, sneaking it, not sharing it, doing it by myself, not wanting to see anyone else. Not wanting to go to work, not caring about commitments to clients.

It's a real fixation. And it takes a physical toll as well. I was balancing an extremely stressful job where it had been hard to keep my health anyway—sleeping on the sofa at work and that kind of stuff—and then adding this. Some days I could feel my heart literally caving in.

I moved myself and my bank balance to Ireland some time later to escape the madness. A board member that I regularly partied with in the us brought me over to work for a venture capital company. For about nine months I kept my nose clean, but then someone finally broke out the coke in front of me one night in Dublin and it felt like seeing an old girlfriend again. It was like the familiar smell or taste of an old flame, you know, of an old girl-friend that you might have fought with all the time, but the sex was so great that you stayed and kept forgetting how bad your relationship was during the day.

And then it became pretty dark, pretty quickly, and I was back to doing it on my own and getting paranoid. Right back from nought to sixty overnight. I was thirty-six years old. I was making incredibly good money—my salary was into six figures and I had a very generous expense account. However, the drug use got serious almost immediately and I failed to show up for a few big meetings. I let down two very influential clients, so I was asked to resign. Fired, basically. And given severance pay.

I was unemployed and bored and I had a bonus cheque. Financially, I didn't need to work so I entertained fantastic notions about spending my days playing tennis and reading and getting healthy and living by the sea conjuring up amazing ideas for new ventures. But all I did was snort more coke than I'd have thought possible, for nearly a full month.

And then, out of the blue, I was headhunted by a large British company in London to launch an online casino, which is about the worst thing the doctor could have prescribed for me. But of course I grabbed it with both hands. It was just too fascinating to even contemplate turning it down for my greater good. You have to remember that nothing was working online except porn and gambling, in terms of entertainment and media. And now instead of lying around the house in Blackrock by myself in a tracksuit, I'm back in the game getting to work with billionaires and wearing the Gucci gear again. I'm exploring the whole netherworld of high-end James Bond gambling. It was just so over the top, it was unbelievable. Here was an internet project that had a great chance of making money at the fast pace that I was after.

They paid me more money than I had ever been paid before and flew me first-class to Asia and all of that. I certainly had the lifestyle. Tennis and reading were instantly forgotten. I wasn't using as many drugs. I had something else to be interested in. So we launched the thing and we did £130 million turnover in the first year.

After that first year I suppose I became complacent. The buzz had died down and I started into the three-hour lunches here with maybe two bottles of wine and some cognac there, and then on to a drinking club and then 'Sure, let's carry on through the night.' I'd call in 'friends' who didn't deserve to go, and then women and dates and my dealer, and I'd have the Mercedes waiting for me out front to take people whose names I barely knew home in the early hours. Now I was taking a lot of coke. I've no idea how much, but *a lot*. It was the whole thing: box seats at Arsenal, lines of coke across the tables after the games, really heavy stuff. I was loving it for a while and I had no qualms about the fact that what I was doing for a living was marketing an addiction. I was well aware of it, of course, but I didn't care.

Anyway, in the second year, I called in sick one too many times and my boss—who was a very astute reader of people—sacked me. Well, he allowed me the dignity to say 'I resign' before he said 'I'm sacking you,' and so I got another cheque.

I was unemployed again, using coke alone at home by the bucket-ful, with time and money to spare. Apart from the drugs, my days involved fiddling with my guitar, flipping through channels on the TV, calling people and making plans that never materialised, writing emails and then going back to fiddling with the guitar.

A good friend knocked on my door one day at five o'clock in the afternoon. I was in a dreadful state, coked up to the eyeballs. This friend is a cardiac surgeon, and he shows up and tells me that I need to think about how much coke I'm using and he starts to talk to me about addiction, and then, out of nowhere, I started to cry. Like a baby, and for a long time.

I decided I was going to use my most recent cheque to pay for three weeks rehab in the US. I went to a boot camp, for want of a better expression, in Arizona—a treatment place called Cottonwood. It was just under $1,000 a day, four people to a room. They confiscate all your stuff and treat you like a misbehaving child. Needless to say, I didn't take to it.

I wrote a letter to them called 'Constructive Criticism' on my third day, which was eighteen pages long, and—wearing my 'Analyse a Business and How it's Run' hat—I asked, among other things, why there were four people to a room. They claimed it was for therapeutic reasons. I think we all know better—four cots in a room for that money!

In my room there was a General from the marine corps, an actor from Hollywood, and a fourth guy I don't recall. The place was full of Indians from the reservations because addiction is such a problem—the casinos pay for rehab for their staff, and then back into the casino with you to do your work and get addicted all over again. There was also a mix of people like myself who were paying for it all themselves, and others who had insurance covering it. We were a mix of men and women with gambling or drink or drug addictions. Or a combination of two or all three.

My family arrived and we did one week of Jerry Springer-esque group family therapy. I will admit that I learned one lasting thing: the meaning of the word 'boundaries' and how I didn't want my family within mine. The therapy would involve us all sitting in a circle and me saying something like, 'Mum, the thing I value most about you is . . . and the thing that has really upset me the most is . . . .' She would then have to say, 'May I give you some advice son?' and I'd have to either say yes or no and so on, for an eternity. We did all of this and then the other people present would give feedback as to how we had done.

At first it was horrible for all of us, but then it seemed to work and we were hugging and crying and all 'Thank God we did this' until the final sentence out of my parents' mouths: 'You are not welcome back in any of our homes nor do we want to see you until you are six months clean.' This was a bit of a kick in the face for me what with all the tears and the hugging that had just gone on.

The staff at Cottonwood wanted me to stay another three weeks but I thought about it and $1,000 a day times three weeks, eating horrible cafeteria food, and watching people chain-smoke nervously ... I'd had enough.

So I left against their advice and without the support of my parents. I hated that the first step of my new life was under so much cloud, but also I felt I had to trust myself and get out of there. So I went to Florida and stayed for a couple of months at a place that a friend owned. I was scared with every step I took. 'When is it going to come back and haunt me?' I never thought it would just stop. The obsession. The constant thoughts and longing.

I haven't used coke since the day I signed myself out of Cottonwood last year, so I suppose it did work on one level. Or maybe it just made me determined not to ever have to go back . . .

In recent weeks, I haven't felt that ex-girlfriend perfume thing any more. In fact I almost experience a physical nausea when I think about what it felt like going down the back of my throat, and my heartbeat accelerating, and then immediately starting to drink and smoke and act like an ass. That said, I don't socialise at night now at all. I don't put myself in the way of temptation.

Dublin has this civilised veneer and it doesn't come in on you immediately like New York does, with all the skyscrapers and the endless concrete. But Dublin is an intense city in its own way and it has its own dark underbelly too. I think it has become very much based on wealth and power and status, without being as honest about it as New York is. Drug use in Ireland is just as rife now as anywhere else, and just as seedy. The perceived glamour of the coke scene is pretty lame and very thin.

I think it is a very rare person who can just get high once a month on a Saturday, you know, with his or her loved one and then wake up on Sunday, have breakfast and read the paper before going back to bed. I really wish I could be that person.

Epilogue

Darcey Clarke and her husband **Matt** live in Dublin. He still practises medicine.

Emma McCarthy is on leave from her position in the maternity hospital. She has had to accept that recovery is too difficult for her in a hospital environment. She is currently taking a course in Public Relations and is considering a career change in the future. Her husband Mark is very pleased about this.

Marian recently started smoking heroin for the first time. She is surprised herself as she always considered it a 'drug of the underclass, but it's not any more. It has become quite popular at my events over the last while. Only smoking it, mind. Not injecting. The high lasts a lot longer than with coke.' Her business is booming.

Alan spends his days reading, writing jingles, 'thinking too much and avoiding getting married'.

Aoife's husband **Ian** is now using cocaine again, after four years in recovery. Aoife is heartbroken and worried for herself and their marriage. 'I have to be selfish now and keep myself strong. I don't know what this will mean for our relationship. I'm determined not to fall again. I wanted to have a baby, but I have to put those plans to one side now.'

Niall is making arrangements to spend another three weeks at Forest soon. He is managing to get by on only the prescribed amount of pain relief for his condition, but finding it 'desperately hard'. He has taken some time off work. His wife Jane is talking about moving out for a while.

Peter is now a Sponsor for three people in Narcotics Anonymous. He feels ready for a 'gentle relationship' and is 'keeping his good eye out' for a nice woman.

Tom and **Eileen** are still hosting their popular dinner parties. They had fourteen people over to ring in New Year 2007. That evening, the gathered group spent €1,900 on cocaine and €470 on ketamine.

Liam Jones is very excited to be expecting a baby with his partner, but also worried about being a bad father and a bad example. He finds the anxiety gets on top of him most days. He is attending NA meetings more frequently at the moment—five times a week—to see him through.

Jane Feeney continues to make every effort to contact her daughter and grandchild. She remains quietly hopeful.

Julian confesses that he is using more drugs 'than is probably advisable'. He is currently living in a Dublin city-centre hotel.

Susan was 'asked to leave' her job with the legal firm. She had an interview with a new company last Friday, but missed it. She has rescheduled another one for this Thursday and is determined to be there and to make a good impression. She is still using cocaine, but her attitude to it has changed. She cried on the phone about her fears that she might be addicted.

Fintan and James are planning to move to Kinsale full-time in June. Fintan intends spending the summer days on his boat and will take up a legal post in Cork in September.

Karl is still using cocaine several days a week and has no plans to stop. He is trying his best 'not to be a dickhead' though.

Fiona was impossible to locate. The production company she is currently contracted to in London is interested in hearing from her.

Kieran left Dublin in December 2006 to return to the US, having been offered an exciting business opportunity in New York. He is determined not to be lured into the city's 'narcotic underbelly'. His eventual ambition is to open a Drug Treatment Centre—'which respects its clients'—in New York state.